King's Fund Institute

KT-577-915

Health Check

Health care reforms in an international context

Chris Ham

Ray Robinson

Michaela Benzeval

DISPOSED OF
BY LIBRARY
HOUSE OF LORDS

©1990 King's Fund Institute

All rights reserved. No part of this publication may be reproduced, stored in any retrieval system, or transmitted, in any form or by any means, electronic, mechanical, photocopying, recording, or otherwise, without the prior permission of the King's Fund Institute.

Published by the King's Fund Institute
126 Albert Street, London NW1 7NF.
Telephone 01-485 9589

Design & print by Intertype
Cover photo: Simon Walker/*Nursing Times*

Contents

Acknowledgments

We are grateful to the Transport and General Workers' Union which provided a grant towards the costs of this study. We would also like to thank the experts who wrote papers for us on four of the countries we have examined: Cornelia Behrens (West Germany), Bob Evans (Canada), Frans Rutten and Eddy van Doorslaer (Holland), and Richard Saltman (Sweden). We have drawn on these papers extensively in the chapters which follow.

Valuable assistance and comments have been provided by the following individuals: Jean-Pierre Poullier, Klaus-Dirk Henke, Douglas Webber, Edgar Borgenhammar, Johan Calltorp, Aad de Roo, Nigel Weaver, Maureen Dixon, Frank Sloan, Gordon Moore, Jonathan Weiner and Rosemary Taylor.

Within the King's Fund, a number of colleagues have helped us to clarify our arguments, in particular Ken Judge, Robert Maxwell, Tony Dawson and Sholom Glouberman.

Finally, we would like to thank the staff of the King's Fund Centre library, and our secretaries — Fiona Helmer, Ann O'Reilly, Sara McDavid and Georgina Stanley — who have word processed successive drafts.

Chris Ham
Ray Robinson
Michaela Benzeval

January 1990

Technical note

Price and expenditure data in the country chapters are presented in the currency of the country concerned and sterling equivalents are noted in parenthesis. These data were converted to sterling at January 1990 exchange rates and were rounded up or down in order to give a broad indication of the sums involved. Information on health expenditure expressed as a proportion of gross domestic product and on the public and private shares of total expenditure are drawn from OECD sources. This information is collected by the OECD on a consistent basis to enable comparisons to be made between countries.

Foreword

There has been a major information gap in the public debate about the performance of the British NHS. The debate has been dominated by comparisons with the USA experience, with little in the way of easily available information about how other countries run their health services, so this report should be welcomed simply for undertaking to overcome this deficiency.

It will also be valued for its scrutiny of some of the questions of reform proposed by the government for our embattled NHS, while its openness of approach stands in stark contrast to the secrecy of method and purpose with which the government conducted its recent NHS policy review.

While the views expressed are those of the King's Fund authors, the spotlight on the funding shortfall is unambiguous and very much to be welcomed. The discussions of quality delivery and management structure draw on a range of approaches to efficiency questions which provide an essential background for debate about the role that patients' rights might be able to play in providing an incentive for a top class service. The concept of 'managed competition' may be too restrictive to cope with legitimate questions of strategic goals for health systems. It cannot surely be separated from questions of popular and customer democracy.

The survey of questions of access should serve to remind readers and policy makers of the unique achievement of the NHS in providing a comprehensive service for all citizens which is free at the point of need.

But, above and beyond these issues are serious challenges from the rising pressures of an ageing British population, the costs of high technology medicine and the difficulty of administering effective preventative strategies alongside the treatment services of the system. These questions require the fullest possible debate about the structure and policy setting of the NHS, and once again, this report shows that the agenda here can be quite open.

Without a clear grasp of the structure issues, progress on the many acute problems of the NHS' patients and workforce will be limited. While the report touches on issues about the role of doctors, I believe that study would be rewarded by the comparative treatment of non-medical staff and community staff in other countries, for they too are a vital ingredient in the equation of good health care.

The test of good analysis is its ability to raise the level of understanding available to public debate. Clearly, this report fulfils this essential requirement, and justifies the assistance given by the Transport and General Workers' Union with the research. Different groups of users will make varied uses of the findings. For our part, I am confident it will allow my union's members to be better informed about the structures which employ their fellow service workers in other countries.

For one thing is certain, it is that the debate about the best road ahead for our National Health Service cannot be conducted solely within a national framework.

Ron Todd
General Secretary, Transport and General Workers' Union

Introduction

This book seeks to illuminate and inform debate about the future of the NHS by reviewing the financing and delivery of health services in a number of developed countries. In writing the book, our main aim has been to identify the strengths and weaknesses of health services in the countries studied, to draw parallels with the UK, and to establish the lessons, if any, from abroad. Our analysis has taken place against the background of the Prime Minister's Review of the NHS, and the resulting white paper, Working for Patients (Secretary of State for Health and others, 1989). At a time when health services in the UK are in a state of flux, we have used comparative analysis to locate the problems confronting the NHS within a broader context.

The countries chosen for study are Sweden, Holland, West Germany, the United States and Canada. These countries were selected because they illustrate different approaches to the financing and delivery of health services. In broad terms, the United States relies principally on private insurance, West Germany and Holland on compulsory social insurance supplemented by private insurance, and Canada and Sweden on taxation. Furthermore, levels of expenditure , expressed as a proportion of gross domestic product, vary from around 8 per cent to over 11 per cent. As well as these differences in funding, each country has adopted a distinctive approach to health care delivery, ranging from government planning through regulation of budgets, prices and fees, to competitive markets.

In reviewing the experience of these countries, we have examined the extent to which the difficulties that have occurred in the UK might be tackled through greater reliance on policy instruments used overseas. In the case of finance, this involves assessing alternative methods of funding, and also the argument for increasing the amount of money raised through taxation. In the case of delivery, it entails reviewing the impact of competition among providers on overall expenditure and efficiency, and examining the experience of regulation and government planning in countries where the role of central government in the organisation of health services is more limited than in the UK.

In addition, we have wherever possible assessed the commitment that exists in these countries to public health and healthy public policy. As the contribution of health services to improvements in health is increasingly recognised to be limited, there has been renewed interest in the social, economic, and environmental influences on health. In view of this interest, we have drawn out the implications for UK policy makers of the approaches taken in different countries and have sought to identify what needs to be done if higher priority is to be given to public health.

It is important to emphasise at the outset that a study such as this rarely produces simple recommendations or lessons. While we have sought to examine the performance of different systems in terms of overall cost control, efficiency in service delivery, equity in access to services and responsiveness to consumers, the evidence we have assembled illustrates the complexities facing policy makers in balancing these considerations. In the final chapter, we bring together the various strands of our analysis and compare and contrast the UK with the countries we have examined. In so doing, we highlight a number of specific points, such as the under investment in health services in the UK, and the widespread interest that exists in managing clinical activity more effectively. However, many of our findings are more general in character and cannot be translated into clear prescriptions for implementation. In no country is there complete satisfaction with the chosen methods of finance and delivery, and there is continuing debate about alternative approaches. In this sense, comparative analysis is more helpful in illustrating the problems that are common to different systems and the variations in policy responses than in suggesting solutions that can be transplanted between systems.

The Plan of the Book

The book is organised as follows. Chapter 1 traces the origins of the Prime Minister's Review of the NHS in order to provide a context for the chapters on individual countries which follow. It shows how cumulative underfunding of the NHS during the 1980s resulted in a severe financial crisis in Autumn 1987. The subsequent debate about the future of the NHS is outlined, and the main proposals of Working for Patients are summarised.

Chapters 2 — 6 review experience in the countries we have selected for study. For each country, we have collected basic information about methods and levels of funding, the ownership of hospitals and other health care facilities, the employment status of doctors, and the policies pursued to control expenditure. In addition, we have examined particular themes in more detail, selecting the themes according to their importance in the country concerned and their relevance for the emerging debate in the UK. As a consequence, the contents of each chapter are slightly different, reflecting the themes we have chosen to highlight in individual countries.

A major concern in chapter 2 is the effectiveness of the Swedish health service in meeting the needs of its population given a level of spending that is high by international standards. In many respects, Sweden has the health service that is most similar to the NHS among all the countries studied, with public finance and public provision predominant. With expenditure at over 9 per cent of GDP, Sweden illustrates what might be possible if spending on the NHS were to be increased significantly. In practice, as our analysis shows, the Swedish health service faces problems with waiting lists for some treatments, a lack of responsiveness to consumers, and an over-emphasis on institutional care. On the other hand, considerable progress has been made in involving doctors in management, there has been a major investment in the assessment of health care technology, and government has provided a strong lead in the development of public health policies. Although radical reform of health services is not on the agenda, various proposals are under debate to overcome the weaknesses of existing arrangements, and these are discussed to assess their relevance for the UK.

Chapters 3 and 4 examine Holland and West Germany respectively, the two countries in our study which rely mainly on social insurance funding. Although the government has rejected alternative methods of funding for the time being, it may well be that the case for switching towards social insurance will again move onto the agenda, particularly if public expenditure constraints remain tight. It therefore seems pertinent to examine the experience of those countries which rely on social insurance to establish the possible implications for the UK.

Chapter 3 focuses particularly on the reforms proposed in Holland by the Dekker report. These reforms bear a strong resemblance to the government's plans for the NHS. The background to the Dekker report is outlined, and the proposals to introduce a more market-oriented approach are discussed. Holland has always had a large measure of pluralism in its health services and this is likely to increase as the Dekker report is implemented. In Chapter 4, the experience of West Germany is assessed. The German social insurance scheme is comprehensive in terms of the services covered, and there is a plentiful supply of doctors and hospital beds. However, there is concern at the upward movement of insurance contributions required to fund health services, and increasing evidence that resources are not always used efficiently. The measures taken by government to control expenditure are discussed, including the most recent health reforms introduced in January 1989.

Chapter 5 reviews the performance of health services in the United States. As the country which has depended most heavily in the past on private insurance and a market in health care, the US is often seen as a model by critics of the NHS (see, for example, Green, 1986). In fact, as we show, health services in the United States are a paradox of excess and deprivation. There are extreme inequalities in access to health care, and those who are uninsured or under insured have to fall back on whatever is available in the residual public system. Despite these deficiencies, US experience of competition between providers and of managed health care is highly relevant to the government's plans for the NHS. We summarise the available evidence on these issues , and also discuss the approach taken to technology assessment and health services accreditation.

Canada's health services, discussed in chapter 6, provide a valuable counterpoint to the United States. All hospital and medical services are provided through public financing and resources are raised through taxation. Expenditure is considerably lower than in the United States and access to health care is excellent. Furthermore, the evidence suggests a high level of satisfaction with health services among the Canadian people and little desire for major change. Tensions and problems do exist, but in many respects health services in Canada appear to have avoided the weaknesses which have emerged elsewhere.

Finally, chapter 7 draws together the elements of the analysis and compares the UK with the countries studied. The chapter emphasises that there are no quick-fix solutions to the problems faced by the health care systems of developed countries. Although there are some clear lessons from international experience, in general it is the complexity and intractability of policy dilemmas in the health services field that is most striking.

Audience

The audience for the book includes those with policy making responsibilities, academics and researchers, and general readers who are seeking a better appreciation of the options for the future. On the assumption that readers will have variable amounts of knowledge about the systems we have studied, each of the country chapters begins with a description of the principal features of the system concerned and presents key facts and figures. This is followed by an analysis of issues such as expenditure control, the efficiency of service delivery, the extent of consumer choice, and the management of clinical activity. Each chapter ends with a summary of strengths and weaknesses and a brief commentary on the country under analysis. Chapter 7 synthesises our major findings and highlights points of similarity and difference in the evidence we have reviewed. Specialist readers may prefer to begin with chapter 7 and return to the country chapters to explore particular themes in greater depth.

1 The NHS Review: origins and outcome

For much of its history, the NHS has appeared to be in a permanent state of crisis. In a widely quoted passage, Enoch Powell, Minister of Health between 1960 and 1963, observed that:

> One of the most striking features of the National Health Service is the continual, deafening chorus of complaint which rises day and night from every part of it, a chorus only interrupted when someone suggests that a different system altogether might be preferable, which would involve the money coming from some less (literally) palpable source. The universal Exchequer financing of the service endows everyone providing as well as using it with a vested interest in denigrating it, so that it presents what must be a unique spectacle of an undertaking that is run down by everyone engaged in it (1976, p.16).

The chorus of complaint to which Powell refers has continued unabated since he left office, despite significant increases in expenditure, staff employed and patients treated.

Recognition of the recurrent nature of NHS crises suggests that any particular outburst of complaint should be treated with caution. Nevertheless, it did appear that the funding position entered an acute phase in the autumn of 1987. Health authorities found that expenditure was running rapidly ahead of cash allocations and many were required to take urgent action to ensure that they did not overspend their budgets.

A survey of 106 health authorities carried out by the National Association of Health Authorities (NAHA) reported that health authorities throughout England were under considerable financial pressure. Various measures were being taken to cope with these pressures including drawing on reserves, transferring cash from capital to revenue and delaying payments to creditors. In addition, staff vacancies were frozen, wards were closed on a temporary basis, and non-emergency admissions were cancelled (NAHA, 1987).

The financial pressures facing health authorities were compounded by staff shortages. In particular, difficulties were experienced in recruiting specialist nurses to work in intensive therapy units. In this case, overall financial constraints were not the main cause of the problem. However, the effect on services to patients was much the same in that operations were cancelled and waiting lists lengthened. Public discussion of this issue focused on Birmingham Children's Hospital where the shortage of specialist nurses meant that a number of children had their heart operations delayed. The parents of two of these children, David Barber and Mathew Collier, resorted to legal action in an attempt to bring the operations forward, but to no avail.

Doctors as well as patients became increasingly vocal in drawing attention to the impact of cash and staff shortages on hospital services. Two events of particular importance occurred in December 1987. First, the BMA issued a statement claiming that the funding of hospital services was seriously inadequate and that additional resources were required to meet the real needs of the acute sector. Second, the Presidents of the Royal Colleges of Surgeons, Physicians and Obstetricians and Gynaecologists issued a joint statement claiming that the NHS had almost reached breaking point and that additional and alternative financing had to be provided.

In the face of mounting public and professional concern, the government announced in December 1987 that an additional £101 million was to be made available in 1987/8 in the UK to help ameliorate the problems that had arisen. At around the same time, details were released of the new clinical grading structure for nurses and midwives. One of the aims of the new structure was to attract nurses into specialist areas of work where shortages existed. In the short term, these measures did little to relieve the pressure on the government, and as a consequence the Prime Minister decided to initiate a fundamental review of the NHS. The decision was revealed during an interview on the BBC TV programme, Panorama, on 25 January 1988, and it was made clear that the results would be published within a year.

The Origins of the Funding Crisis

If funding crises can make a claim to be the occupational disease of the NHS, what was so distinctive about the problems that emerged in the autumn of 1987? And why did the funding crisis develop when it did? The reasons are complex but the essence of the explanation can be found through an examination of recent NHS expenditure trends.

During the 1980s, the NHS has operated within the context of extremely tight public expenditure controls. Cash limits have been applied far more stringently than in the past, and pay awards have not always been fully funded. Hospital services have been particularly severely constrained with spending in purchasing power terms increasing by an average rate of only just over 0.5 per cent per year since 1980 (Robinson et al., 1988). In the same period, the demand for health care has been rising because of increasing numbers of elderly people in the population and advances in medical technology. The finance required to meet these demands is greater than the cash made available. As a consequence, a funding shortfall has arisen, and this is illustrated in Figure 1.

Figure 1   Hospital and Community Health Services: Trends in Spending, Targets and Shortfalls

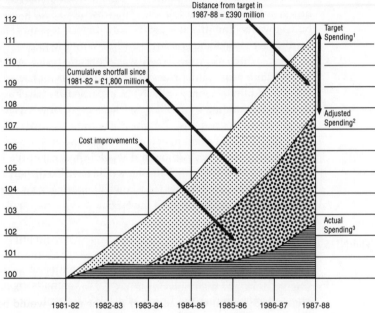

Source: Robinson *et al* (1983)

Notes

1   Increase over base spending necessary for demography, technology and service improvements: 1.3 to 2.3 per cent per year.

2   Actual spending plus cash releasing cost improvements at 1987-88 purchasing power prices.

3   Actual spending at 1987-88 purchasing power prices

It would appear that the funding crisis of autumn 1987 was the result of cumulative underfunding. Moreover it was becoming increasingly difficult to offset shortfalls in core funding through internally generated savings. As Figure 1 shows, health authorities had already realised significant efficiency savings in the 1980s through cost improvement programmes. These programmes contributed an estimated £408 million to the hospital and community health services budget in England by the end of March 1987. By 1987, however, the clear view expressed by health authorities and key professional groups was that the scope for further savings was narrowing considerably.

A further complication was that staff working in hospitals were faced with the perverse phenomenon of being penalised for their own success. This occurred because treating an increasing number of patients — at lower costs per patient — often resulted in additional total expenditure for which there was no extra income. Caught in the so called 'efficiency trap', health authorities found that the only way they could keep within their budget was to limit the amount of work done. It was for this reason that wards were closed and waiting list admissions cancelled.

Against this background, there was a concerted call from organisations representing health authorities, staff and patients for the government to allocate additional money to the NHS, in particular to the hospital service, to tackle the funding shortfall. As we have noted, this was indeed part of the government's response. But the Prime Minister clearly decided that a more fundamental examination of the financing and provision of health services was required. Although it would appear that the Review took place sooner than the Prime Minister would have liked, there is little doubt that the funding crisis provided a convenient trigger for a wide-ranging re-examination of the future of the NHS.

The NHS Review

The Prime Minister established a small committee of senior ministers chaired by herself to conduct the Review. The committee met in Downing Street, demonstrating the Prime Minister's determination to be closely involved and to control the outcome. A support group of civil servants and political advisers (including members of the Prime Minister's Policy Unit) prepared papers for the committee. As an internal review, there was no public invitation to bodies such as the BMA and the Royal Colleges to submit papers, although a wide range of organisations took the opportunity to express their views in public through conferences and publications.

A key development which occurred during the Review was the decision to split the DHSS into two and to move John Moore to the new Department of Social Security. Following an illness, Moore struggled to control one of the biggest departments in government. Before his departure, Moore signalled his intention to pursue a path of evolutionary reform, and this was reinforced by the appointment of Kenneth Clarke as the new Secretary of State for Health. As a firm supporter of the NHS, Clarke was well placed to develop a series of proposals designed to introduce reforms within the framework of continuing public financing of health services. At the same time, his appointment delayed the completion of the Review. In the event, it was not until 31 January 1989 that the results were published in a white paper, Working for Patients. What then were the main issues that the year long review highlighted?

Despite significant differences between the contributors to the debate about the direction reform should take, there was a wide measure of agreement on the nature of the problems to be tackled. As many commentators pointed out, viewed in the international context the NHS provided good value for money. Total expenditure on health care, at around 6 per cent of GDP, was low by comparative standards, and yet for this spending, the entire population had access to comprehensive services of a generally high standard. Furthermore, most services were available on the basis of need and not ability to pay and patients were not deterred from seeking treatment by a price barrier. Comprehensive planning of services meant that all parts of the country had access to health care; and a well developed system of primary care resulted in many medical problems being dealt with by GPs without the need to refer patients to hospitals. All this was achieved with only a small proportion of the budget being spent on administration.

Set against these strengths, it was widely acknowledged that the NHS had a number of weaknesses. Tight control of expenditure by government had resulted in under funding of health services and this was evident in the state of the capital stock, waiting lists for some forms of treatment, and the poor quality of care provided for the priority groups. Funding constraints also meant that pay rates had been held down and this had given rise to recruitment difficulties. Variations in performance between health authorities indicated that resources were not always used optimally and there were few incentives for efficiency. Furthermore, patients had limited choice of services and those responsible for planning and management did not always take account of patients' demands. The division of responsibility for primary care, community care and hospital services hindered the integrated planning and delivery of services and created perverse incentives for service providers. And within the NHS as a whole, the provision of health services was given higher priority than the promotion of health.

During the Review, a wide variety of ideas were put forward for tackling the weaknesses of the NHS. In broad terms, these ideas centred on two questions: how should health care be financed? And how should health care be delivered?

The Financing Debate

The debate about financing dominated the early stages of the Review. Three main themes emerged. First, a number of organisations argued that there was no need to change the basis of funding the NHS through general taxation. This argument was based on the view that the NHS had performed reasonably well when judged against its founding principles. Those who supported this view maintained that the problems confronting the NHS could be tackled most effectively by increased public expenditure and supplementary sources of finance such as income generation.

The second theme was that the service should continue to be publicly financed but that funds should be raised through social insurance rather than general taxation. One of the principal advocates of this view was Leon Brittan (1988). His argument was that social insurance would establish greater transparency between payments and spending. According to Brittan, people would be willing to pay more for health care if the relationship between their contributions and the total level of NHS expenditure were more visible. Brittan also argued that a financing system based on social insurance would enable individuals who registered with a private scheme to opt out of the state social insurance scheme.

Brittan's views had clear links to the third theme which was that there should be a substantial increase in private expenditure on health care. Various ideas were put forward for encouraging individuals to spend more on health care. Apart from opting out of social insurance, the main proposal was that the government should extend tax relief to those with private health insurance cover. It was argued that this would provide an incentive for people to use the private sector, thereby reducing the demands made on the NHS.

The Delivery Debate

The debate about health care delivery focused mainly on ways of encouraging competition and strengthening professional accountability. As the Review developed, the debate about delivery assumed greater importance and discussion of alternative forms of financing took a back seat. The main reason for this appeared to be uncertainty on the part of those conducting the Review about whether radical changes to the method of funding health services would help tackle the problems facing the NHS.

The original argument in favour of greater competition was put forward by Alain Enthoven well before the Prime Minister's Review (Enthoven, 1985). Enthoven's proposal that an internal market should be established within the NHS was developed in a number of ways. Of particular interest were the Adam Smith Institute's advocacy of Health Management Units (HMUs)(Butler and Pirie,1988) and the idea of Managed Health Care Organisations (MHCOs) put forward by the Centre for Policy Studies (Goldsmith and Willetts, 1988). Both proposals drew on US experience of Health Maintenance Organisations. In the case of HMUs, it was envisaged that individuals would register with a GP who in turn would register with a HMU. The function of a HMU would be to purchase the necessary secondary and community care for its patients.

In the case of MHCOs, it was envisaged that individuals would register with the MHCO which would choose the necessary primary, secondary and community care for them. In both cases, funding would be provided to the HMU/MHCO by the Department of Health, with the HMU/MHCO acting as a purchasing agent on behalf of patients. This would force hospitals to compete for business from the HMU/MHCO.

The other main theme in the delivery debate was that the accountability of doctors should be strengthened. Submissions from a wide range of organisations drew attention to the need to manage clinical activity more effectively. Proposals in this area included extending medical audit, involving doctors in management and giving doctors more responsibility for budgets. It was also argued that the contractual position of doctors should be modified, particularly in the hospital service, to ensure that managers were able to exercise effective control over clinical work.

Apart from these themes, a number of other issues relating to delivery arose during the Review. For example, several organisations put forward proposals designed to improve the planning and management of services. These proposals included clarifying the management of the NHS at the centre, merging the responsibilities of DHAs and FPCs, and refashioning the role of health authorities. Other submissions argued that the Griffiths general management reforms should be strengthened to enable inefficiencies to be tackled more directly and to introduce a stronger consumer orientation. In parallel, there was continuing discussion about the future of community care, and concern that any changes to the NHS should help to promote the better use of resources in this area.

The White Paper

In the white paper, the government announced that the basic principles on which the NHS was founded would be preserved. Funding would continue to be provided mainly out of taxation and there were no proposals to extend user charges. Tax relief on private insurance premiums was to be made available to those aged over 60, apparently at the Prime Minister's insistence, but the significance of this was more symbolic than real. For the vast majority of the population, access to health care was to be based on need and not ability to pay.

The main changes heralded by the white paper concerned the delivery of health care. In the case of GPs, the government announced that practices would be encouraged to advertise and to provide more information about their services. GPs' remuneration was to be based mainly on the number of patients served, to encourage GPs to be more responsive to patients, and it was to be made easier for patients to change GPs to ensure that real choice could be exercised in practice.

In the case of hospitals, funding was to be based on service contracts and hospitals would be reimbursed for the work done. Again, this was intended to create an incentive to hospitals to attract patients. More importantly, the white paper emphasised the need to develop competition between hospitals. To achieve this, the funding of services by health authorities was to be increasingly separated from their provision. Acting on behalf of their communities, health authorities would purchase services from a range of public, private and voluntary providers. These providers would include hospitals which opted out of health authority control to become self-governing institutions within the NHS. At the same time, larger GP practices would be able to volunteer to hold a budget for certain hospital services for their patients. Like health authorities, GPs were expected to shop around on behalf of their patients for these services.

The central proposals of the white paper were intended to create the conditions for managed competition in the health services. By introducing market principles, the government hoped not only to make services more responsive to patients, but also to stimulate greater efficiency in the use of resources. And by insisting that competition should be managed, the government sought to ensure that the basic principles of the NHS would not be undermined by a more businesslike approach.

Two other ideas lay at the heart of the white paper, both concerned with delivery rather than finance. The first was the proposal that doctors should be made more accountable for their performance. To this end, the white paper announced that medical audit was to become a routine part of general practice and clinical work in hospitals; job descriptions for hospital consultants were to be tightened; general managers were to be involved in appointing consultants and in decisions about merit awards; and revised disciplinary procedures were to be introduced for hospital doctors. Alongside these changes, the resource management initiative was to be rapidly extended throughout the NHS to ensure that hospital doctors were more closely involved in the management of services.

The second idea was that management should be strengthened. Here the white paper endorsed the Griffiths general management reforms and took them a stage further by proposing to refashion the role of health authorities along the lines of boards of directors. The management of the NHS at the centre was also to be clarified with the establishment of a new Policy Board and Management Executive. More generally, the white paper argued that responsibility for management should be delegated to as local a level as possible and that management should be given greater flexibility within overall guidelines set from above.

A number of key issues were not addressed in the white paper. Foremost among these was public health and the role of health promotion within the NHS. It would seem that the government was concerned principally with the problems of acute hospitals and the relationship between hospital services and GPs, rather than broader aspects of health policy.

The white paper was also silent on the question of additional funding for the NHS. The issue which sparked the Review was therefore not tackled, and this promised to store up problems for a later date. As we show in the following chapters, health services spending in the UK is low when compared with other developed countries, and critics of the government were not slow to point this out in their campaigns for additional resources.

The Relevance of International Comparisons

As the outcome of the most fundamental review of the NHS since its inception, Working for Patients provided an important endorsement of the public financing of health care through taxation. Yet in proposing major changes to the delivery of services, the white paper held out the prospect of considerable upheaval and turbulence during the 1990s. The agenda for change posed a formidable challenge to those responsible for managing and providing services, not least because of the rapid pace of implementation envisaged by the government.

During the Review, many commentators used experience from other countries to suggest how the NHS might be reformed. Particular emphasis was placed on the United States which was held up as an example of a country with a health care system in which patients had choice and where competition between providers created incentives for efficiency. Although there is a clear flavour of United States experience in the white paper, there has been no unthinking acceptance of the health care system of any one country. Rather, the government's programme of reform is an amalgam of initiatives already underway within the UK and ideas under discussion or in operation in a number of other countries.

In view of the mixed origins of Working for Patients, we have drawn on experience from Sweden, Holland, West Germany, and Canada, as well as the United States, to identify parallels with the UK and to establish the lessons, if any, from abroad. As we emphasised in the Introduction, our aim has been less to find examples that can be transplanted to the UK than to be clear about the problems that are common to different systems and the variety of policy responses to these problems. This book is thus in the tradition of Maxwell (1981), McLachlan and Maynard (1982), OECD (1987) and other authors who have used comparative analysis to illuminate the choices facing policy makers. In locating the analysis firmly in the context of the Prime Ministers' Review and Working for Patients, we hope that our findings will be particularly relevant to continuing debate about the future of the NHS.

2 Sweden

Sweden is a country which attaches high priority to the provision of health services in the public sector. Expenditure is above the average for developed countries and resources are raised mainly through national and local taxation. Nearly all hospitals and health service facilities are run by local authorities and Swedish people expect to have access to a full range of services.

For the most part, these expectations are met, although there are waiting lists for some treatments, services are not always organised in a way which is responsive to consumers, and there is concern about the overemphasis placed on institutional care. Within Sweden, there is increasing interest in reforms which will enable these weaknesses to be tackled. Although there has been a growth in private finance and provision in recent years, there is no suggestion that the public sector should be displaced from its dominant role. Rather, the emphasis is on reforming the public sector to enable it to fend off the private sector challenge.

In this chapter, we describe how health services are financed and provided, and discuss the instruments used to control expenditure. The predominance of institutional care is highlighted, and the difficulty of giving greater priority to primary care is noted. Attention then shifts to the initiatives that have been taken to make services more responsive to consumers and to stimulate provider competition. Leading on from this, there is discussion of the management of clinical activity, and of public health policy. Finally, the key strengths and weaknesses of health services in Sweden are summarised.

The Financing and Provision of Services

Health services expenditure comprised 9 per cent of GDP in 1987. Services are overwhelmingly publicly financed with over 90 per cent of expenditure coming from public sources. Expenditures are financed through a combination of general taxation and social insurance.

Taxes are levied at the national, county and municipal levels. Around 70 per cent of public expenditures are met from county and municipal tax revenues with the remainder deriving from social insurance and national tax revenues. Both county and municipal revenues come predominantly from a tax levied as a fixed percentage on the personal income of local residents. Social insurance funds for the health service are raised as part of general social insurance contributions paid by employers for each employee.

Private expenditures include nominal user charges for visiting a doctor, hotel services in hospital (on a daily rate basis) and prescription drugs. In each case, these charges amount to 50 crowns (£5), subject to a maximum of 15 payments each year. In addition, there is a small private insurance sector with an estimated 15,000 policy holders (approximately 0.2 per cent of the population). Nearly all of those covered by private insurance are senior executives whose policies are purchased for them by their employers.

Service delivery is also concentrated in the public sector. The overwhelming majority of hospitals, health centres and other health service facilities are owned and run by the Swedish county councils and the three municipal councils that have responsibility for providing health services. Also, most doctors are salaried employees in the public sector. The small private sector is dominated by nursing home provision. There are approximately 250 privately operated nursing homes in Sweden offering long term care for elderly and mentally ill patients. Many of these are non-profit institutions run by local religious and other organisations. In addition, there are two private hospitals and a small number of privately run health centres and clinics. Around 5 per cent of Swedish doctors are engaged solely in private practice, although Rosenthal (1986) has estimated that as many as 27 per cent may be involved in private work if part time and spare time commitments are included.

Expenditure on health services in Sweden is high by international standards. In part, this reflects Sweden's standard of living. Wealthier countries consistently spend more on health services than poor countries, whatever their method of funding. As one of the world's richest countries, Sweden invests heavily in health care.

Equally important is the high priority attached to health services by Swedish people. Under the leadership of social democratic governments, Sweden has gained an international reputation as a country which has made a major commitment to the development of the welfare state over the last 60 years. This commitment is evident in many areas of Swedish society but nowhere more so than in the health services.

All Swedish citizens are entitled to receive comprehensive health services on the basis of need. No groups in the population are excluded from the health care system. The comprehensive income support arrangements that exist mean that patients are not deterred from seeking treatment by the charges that are levied. Furthermore, Swedish law states clearly that services should be available on an equal basis. Equality of access to health care reflects a broader set of values within the social democratic tradition.

One other factor is relevant in interpreting Swedish expenditure figures, namely the high proportion of elderly people in the population. It is well established that people aged over 65 make heavy use of health services. Of all the countries in our study, Sweden contains the highest proportion in this age group. This helps to explain why spending on health services is comparatively high. Indeed, if expenditure is adjusted to reflect the age structure of the population, then Swedish spending appears to be much closer to that of other developed countries (Landstingsforbundet, 1988).

Expenditure Control

As was noted above, public expenditure on health services derives from county and municipal tax revenues as well as national taxes and social insurance. The key decisions on how much money should be spent rests with the county councils and municipal councils responsible for health services, numbering 26 in total. The management of health services is decentralised to these councils whose independence is based on their ability to levy taxes and the legitimacy which comes from local elections. National government can exert some influence over expenditure through the resources it makes available, but it is at the local level that the ultimate power to determine spending lies.

County councils are able to control expenditure through fixed budgets agreed in advance. These budgets apply to both hospitals and health centres. With certain exceptions (see below), budgets are not varied to take account of workload. As all doctors employed in the public sector are paid on a salaried basis, county councils are able to plan expenditure with a reasonable degree of certainty. Unexpected demands and pressures do arise, but these can usually be accommodated within the budgets allocated.

The existence of what are, in effect, elected health authorities accountable to their communities and with the ability to raise money through taxes is one of the major differences between the UK and Sweden. In the past, the multiplicity of local funding agencies was one of the factors that fuelled the increase in expenditure on health services. This was particularly so in the 1960s and 1970s when county councils competed with each other to expand and modernise their services. Figure 2 illustrates the rising trend in county council taxes between 1960 and 1985. It was only in the 1980s that the rate of increase in taxes and spending slowed significantly.

Figure 2 Swedish County Council Taxes 1960–85

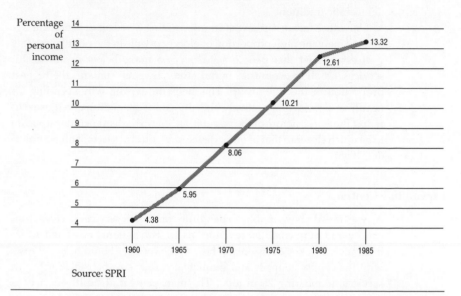

Source: SPRI

The trigger for this slowdown was Sweden's declining economic performance. A balance of payments deficit and an escalating public sector borrowing requirement forced the government to control the growth of public expenditure. Annual negotiations between the Ministry of Finance and the County Councils Federation succeeded in limiting county council tax increases to an agreed level. These agreements remained in operation even after a turnaround in the economy in the mid-1980s. The combination of negotiated limits on health services expenditure and rapid economic growth in more recent years has resulted in a reduction in the percentage of GDP consumed by health care from 9.7 per cent in 1982 to 9 per cent in 1987.

This reduction was the subject of public debate in the run-up to the 1988 election. Out of this debate, a broad consensus emerged that there should be a significant increase in spending on health services. Accordingly, over half the county councils proposed tax increases for 1989 to fund this expansion.

The Predominance of Institutional Care

The expansion of health services that occurred in the post war period was concentrated on the acute hospital sector. As a consequence, there was a significant investment in new hospitals, and a considerable development of specialist services. Much lower priority was given to primary care, although this has begun to change in recent years (see below). In large part, the emphasis given to hospital services can be explained in terms of the high value placed on specialist care. With many patients, politicians and doctors supporting the growth of the acute sector, it was difficult to increase the proportion of expenditure allocated to services outside hospital (Ham, 1987; National Board of Health and Welfare, 1982; 1985). Furthermore, the availability of beds meant that they were used, and this helped to perpetuate the emphasis given to hospital provision.

As a number of studies have shown, Sweden currently spends a high percentage of its health care budget on institutional care, including hospitals. For example, the OECD analysis of the financing and delivery of health care showed that institutional spending comprised 72.6 per cent of total public health spending in Sweden in the 1980s, compared with an OECD mean of 54.2 per cent. In the same period, Sweden provided 14 inpatient beds per 1000 population, compared with an OECD mean of 9.3, although it should be noted that many of these beds were for long-term care. The OECD analysis also demonstrated that Sweden had the highest use of beds of all OECD countries with 4.8 inpatient days per capita (OECD, 1987).

The corollary of a high investment in institutional services has been low expenditure on primary care. As the OECD analysis showed, ambulatory spending comprised 10.2 per cent of total public health spending in the 1980s, compared with a mean of 21.3 per cent. However, priorities have shifted in recent years as the need to contain expenditure has prompted a reappraisal of spending patterns. A report published by the government in 1985 echoed earlier analyses in calling for a change of emphasis to give higher priority to services provided outside hospital (National Board of Health and Welfare, 1985). Expenditure trends in the 1980s indicate that this policy has had some success (OECD, 1987).

Nevertheless, many patients continue to refer themselves directly to hospital rather than going through a GP. Unlike their counterparts in the NHS, Swedish GPs do not act as gatekeepers to the hospital service. This has obvious expenditure implications and is a continuing cause of concern to a government committed to shifting the balance of care away from hospitals.

One other aspect of Swedish health services worth highlighting is the lack of integration between primary care, hospital care and social services. As in the UK, the division of responsibilities between agencies at the local level has hindered the comprehensive planning of services. With county councils responsible for health services, and municipal councils responsible for social services, it has not proved easy to develop an integrated approach to service planning and service provision.

The problems of co-ordinating services across different agencies have been felt most acutely in the case of elderly people. County councils have complained that hospital beds have been blocked because of inadequate social services support. In the absence of such support, many counties have developed nursing homes for the elderly, often in the past in large institutions providing services which are increasingly recognised to be both expensive and inappropriate. This is a further reason why institutional care dominates health services provision. To overcome these problems, an agreement has been reached in principle to transfer responsibility for non-acute care of the elderly from the county councils to the municipal councils in 1992. It is hoped that this will result in the provision of more appropriate and cost effective services, centred on supporting elderly people in their own homes.

Consumer Choice

Despite the high level of investment in acute hospital services, Sweden shares some of the problems of waiting lists for treatment that exist in the NHS. Attention has focused in particular on waiting lists of up to two years for hip replacements, cataract surgery, and coronary artery bypass surgery. In 1987, national government earmarked special funds to tackle this problem. These funds were used by the county councils to provide extra operations themselves, to purchase services from other county councils and from the private sector, and to enable patients to travel for an operation if it could be done more quickly in a hospital outside their area of residence. Included in the scheme was a financial incentive to county councils in the form of a generous reimbursement for operations performed on patients from outside their boundaries.

The national waiting list fund was not continued in 1988 because of objections from the county councils to the use of special earmarked grants. Nevertheless, it is illustrative of a more general concern to respond to patients' demands and to extend patient choice. In the past, choice has been limited with patients expected to use the health centre or hospital near where they live. Also, services have often been organised with the needs of staff rather than patients in mind.

The Social Democratic government, re-elected in 1988, campaigned to extend consumer choice, and this is influencing a range of public services including health. The impact can be seen in more flexible opening hours, the provision of clinics in city centres close to where people work, and the development in Stockholm of a choice for consumers between maternity departments and health centres. The Stockholm maternity services initiative includes a payment system which rewards those hospitals that attract extra patients. In another county, patients who have to wait longer than a specified time for an outpatient appointment have their consultation fee returned.

Through the use of these and other financial incentives, attempts are being made to ensure that services are more responsive to patients. Recent initiatives build on an established system of reimbursing certain hospitals on the basis of the number of patients treated. University hospitals, which are organised regionally, make charges for treatment which are paid by the county council in which patients are resident. Similarly, county hospitals are reimbursed for treating patients from outside their areas according to a national tariff determined by the County Councils Federation. However, the distances involved in travelling to hospital in Sweden have meant that this form of payment plays a limited part in stimulating competition between university and county hospitals.

Linked to these developments, there have been moves to improve the management of services in order to enhance consumer responsiveness. This involves making use of patient satisfaction surveys, undertaking staff training in customer relations and decentralising the planning and management of services to a local level. These initiatives are part of a broader programme of public sector reform aimed at overcoming widely recognised weaknesses in service delivery.

Provider Competition

As we have noted, the private sector in Sweden is small in relation to the public sector. It is also the case that private providers are dependent on the county councils for much of their finance. This applies not only to private hospitals that contract to undertake work for the county councils, but also to doctors practising privately who require county council approval if they are to be reimbursed by the councils for treating patients. Similarly, where health centres have been contracted out to private providers — as in Stockholm and Halland — this has been on the initiative of the county councils.

The private sector has developed in part in response to the failure of the public sector to meet patient and public demands. An example is City Akuten, a walk-in clinic in central Stockholm, providing GP and specialist services on an outpatient basis. The success of this clinic led to the establishment of a county council alternative in 1988 as part of the public sector response to the private sector challenge.

Another reason behind the development of the private sector has been the negotiation of employment contracts for doctors and other staff which provide these staff with generous amounts of spare time. This has resulted in doctors having sufficient time to practise privately out of hours. One of the consequences has been that doctors have organised themselves as private firms to sell back their services to county councils in the evenings and weekends. The staff involved use public hospital facilities for this purpose and are paid according to the amount of work done. This was one of the ways in which action was taken to reduce waiting lists in 1987.

Within the public sector, the idea of public competition as a strategy for responding to patients' demands and increasing efficiency has been gaining currency. The initiative taken in Stockholm to give consumers a choice of maternity services and to reward those hospitals attracting additional women is a practical example of this. Saltman and von Otter (1987, 1989) have spelt out the key elements of public competition, emphasising the role of patients in choosing among publicly employed GPs and hospitals. As Saltman and von Otter note, public competition depends on the existence of financial incentives to reward providers who are successful in attracting patients. The corollary is that GPs and hospitals that fail to attract patients lose out financially. In essence, then, providers compete for a bigger market share within fixed, global budgets. There are clear parallels with the UK government's plans for the NHS.

One aspect of the growing interest in public competition that has particular relevance to the NHS concerns primary care budgets. As in proposals for GP practice budgets, these would cover the cost of certain hospital services as well as primary care. Two counties are actively discussing the introduction of such budgets, although there is as yet no experience of primary care budgets in operation.

Managing Clinical Activity

The principal mechanism for cost containment in Sweden is the use of prospective budgets for hospitals and health centres. With overall expenditure control in this way, little attention has been paid to the way in which resources are used within budgets. As in the NHS, there is a lack of incentives for micro-efficiency in the health care system.

In the case of primary care, GPs have no incentives to reduce their hospital referral rates or to treat borderline cases in primary care. Indeed, with the existence of separate fixed budgets for health centres and hospitals, a health centre is in effect penalised if it seeks to reduce referrals by building up its own services. This is one of the considerations behind the interest shown in primary care budgets covering hospital services as well as GP services.

The high value placed on specialist care in Sweden puts considerable pressure on GPs to refer patients to hospital. Indeed, Swedish citizens have a statutory right to refer themselves to specialists as well as to be seen in a casualty department. The only restrictions on this right are those created by waiting lists. From the GP's perspective, the right of self referral, coupled with the desire to retain credibility with patients in a society which values specialist care more highly than general practice, creates a strong incentive to refer.

The freedom of GPs to refer is limited in two ways. First, in the case of highly specialised services, the patient must usually be seen by a specialist in a county hospital before being examined at a university hospital. Second, GPs are normally required to refer to a hospital within the same county, and often to a single hospital designated to receive patients within that part of the county. These are significant restrictions on both GPs and patients and practices are beginning to change only in response to pressures to increase patient choice.

Within hospitals, consultants manage their own work in much the same way as their colleagues in the NHS. However, an important difference is that in each specialty there is a designated clinic chief (or clinical director) who provides medical leadership. While individual consultants retain the clinical freedom to practise in the way they consider appropriate, the clinic chief provides overall coordination of the work of the clinic and represents his colleagues within the hospital. In this sense, there is a clearer system of medical management in Swedish hospitals than in NHS hospitals.

Recent developments have sought to strengthen the role of clinic chiefs. For example, instead of the most senior doctors taking on this role there is now a move to appoint those clinicians best able to do the job. Furthermore, appointments are increasingly made on a fixed term basis, and county councils have been given greater freedom to set their own pay rates. In parallel, management training for clinicians has expanded.

Linked to these developments, management arrangements within hospitals are being decentralised. This often involves the appointment of a manager and senior nurse to work alongside the clinic chief. In the case of smaller clinics, these staff may support two or more chiefs. Increasingly, too, budgetary responsibility is being delegated to clinics. Clinical budgets, or frame budgets as they are more usually known in Sweden, have existed in some counties since the 1970s, and they are now being introduced on a more widespread basis. Thus, through a combination of measures, steps have been taken to increase incentives for efficiency within hospitals.

The available evidence indicates that these measures have had some success. For example, in a review of experience with frame budgets, Hakansson (1986) reported that staff viewed budgets positively and had become more cost conscious. The savings achieved in the experiments analysed by Hakansson resulted mainly from a reduction in the use of drugs and diagnostic tests and through not filling vacancies.

This conclusion is supported by experience at the Department of Thoracic Medicine at the Karolinska Hospital in Stockholm (Unge, personal communication). With an annual budget of approximately 20 million crowns (£2 million), the Department employs 17 doctors and 80 other staff. The clinic chief runs the Department in association with a manager and a senior nurse. It is expected that the Department will treat an agreed number of patients each year within its budget. If the workload exceeds the target then the budget may be increased but the payments are such that this does not act as a major incentive. More important is the ability to vary items of expenditure within the budget and to retain a proportion of savings.

The Department cannot increase the numbers of doctors employed without the approval of the hospital director and the board of politicians responsible for running the hospital, but otherwise has considerable discretion in the use of the budget. If the budget is underspent, the Department retains 50 per cent of the savings. Changes in clinical practice introduced in the Department include a reduction in diagnostic tests, and a reorganisation of nurse staffing to appoint more qualified nurses and to reduce the number of nursing assistants. In addition, a new computer system has been introduced, and the cleaning of the Department has been contracted out to a private firm.

Although the Department is at the forefront of efforts to manage the use of clinical resources more effectively within hospitals, it is not unique. Similar initiatives have been taken in other counties and there is now considerable pressure to extend these initiatives throughout the health service. However, difficulties have been experienced in persuading managers to move from central hospital administration to work in the clinics, and doctors do not always have the necessary skills or interest in management. Also, there is an active debate about whether nurses as well as doctors can be appointed as chiefs. In one experiment in Vasteras opposition to decentralised management reached the point at which 200 doctors called for the abolition of the new management units (Ievins and Revenas, 1990).

A further difficulty is the absence of reliable information systems to enable clinic chiefs to review activity and to compare the performance of clinics. Efforts are being made to correct this. A government committee is currently reviewing information systems and is examining how data on the quality of care and DRGs might be used to provide a better basis for assessing the efficiency of services. The need for improved information systems was emphasised by Enthoven in his analysis of Swedish health services (Enthoven, 1989). In particular, Enthoven argued that an independent institution was needed to compel the production of information about service effectiveness and efficiency.

Such an institution already exists in part in the form of the Swedish Planning and Rationalisation Institute (SPRI) and the Swedish Council on Technology Assessment in Health Care. SPRI is jointly owned and funded by national government and the county councils and it analyses various aspects of health service performance. Among other activities, SPRI has organised a series of consensus conferences, it has pioneered the application of DRGs, and it has participated in the development of medical care programmes. These programmes, which are sponsored by the National Board of Health and Welfare, contain explicit written standards and guidelines for the planning and provision of services, and they have been prepared for a range of conditions including lower back pain and breast cancer. Each programme is developed in association with local health service staff. However, the evidence suggests that adequate resources have not always been made available to support implementation of the programmes and that programmes vary widely according to who is involved in their preparation (Pine et al., 1988).

The Swedish Council on Technology Assessment in Health Care is of more recent origins, having been established at the end of 1987. It serves as a clearing house on technology assessment and provides information and advice both to national government and the county councils. The Council is an advisory body and it seeks to influence the use of health care technology by sponsoring research and disseminating the results.

Health in Sweden

Swedes enjoy good health by international standards. Infant mortality rates are among the lowest in the OECD countries, life expectancy is among the highest and the quality of life is generally high. There are many reasons why health in Sweden is good, and the provision of comprehensive health services to the whole population is probably a contributory factor. In addition, per capita incomes are high by international standards, there is low unemployment, the tax and welfare system is strongly redistributive, and standards of housing and education are impressive. While the precise contribution of each of these factors is difficult to determine, taken together they create the conditions in which people have the potential to live healthy lives.

Nevertheless, as recent government reports have demonstrated, Sweden still faces significant health problems (National Board of Health and Welfare, 1982 and 1985). These problems derive from hazards in the environment, unhealthy lifestyles and health inequalities related to differences in income and class. In an attempt to address these problems, the government has lent its support to the WHO's Health for All by the Year 2000 strategy. This includes a strong emphasis on the structural and environmental influences on health, a commitment to reduce social class differences in morbidity and mortality, recognition of the need for intersectoral action at both national and local levels, and a policy of supporting public participation in health and health services. These objectives were enshrined in law in 1985 and form the basis of current efforts to build up health services outside the hospitals.

Underlying government policy in this area, as indeed in the approach taken to health services as a whole, is a commitment to care on equal terms for the entire population. Particular attention has been paid to social class inequalities in health. The contribution of lifestyle to illness and disease is not ignored, but greater emphasis is placed on occupational hazards, the influence of unemployment on health, and the impact of the social environment on the well being of individuals and on the opportunities available for participation in social and community activities.

For its part, government has sought to develop healthy public policies through a variety of means:

• control over alcohol consumption through tax increases and by limiting the distribution of alcohol to state-owned off-licences;

• restrictions on tobacco advertising and policies to increase tobacco prices;

• the provision of childcare facilities and parental leave;

• action to reduce road traffic accidents through strict control of drink-driving and segregation of pedestrians and drivers;

• policies to reduce environmental pollution through the use of lead-free petrol and limits to exhaust emissions.

In 1988, the government published a review of progress made toward the WHO's targets and identified newly emerging problems such as AIDS (National Board of Health and Welfare, 1988). As the review noted, the ability of the health care system to respond to health needs was constrained by limits on expenditure in the 1980s. Equally significant were problems of recruiting staff to work in the health and welfare services in the face of competition from other employers. Although there was a commitment to increase expenditure on health services after the 1988 election, the ability of the service to develop was limited by the shortage of personnel. With unemployment low and female participation in the labour force already high, competition for staff was intense. Various options for tackling this problem were under discussion including recruiting staff from overseas, reducing taxes to increase the incentives to work, and extending working hours. A high priority was also attached to the management of human resources. As the health services approached the 1990s, it was this more than any other issue that posed the most significant challenge to policy makers.

Conclusion and Summary

Analysis of health services in Sweden is of interest because Sweden is an example of a country which provides and finances services principally through the public sector and has chosen to invest a much higher proportion of its national income on health services than most other counties. As such, Swedish experience illustrates what might be possible if expenditure on the NHS were to increase significantly, although of course it is unlikely that Swedish experience would be replicated exactly in this country. In summary, the major strengths of the Swedish health service are:

- the provision of comprehensive services to the whole population on the basis of need;

- the commitment to Health for All by the Year 2000 and healthy public policy at national and local levels;

- the investment made in new buildings and the high standard of hospital and health centre accommodation;

- the strong emphasis on democratic control and local accountability in the health services;

- the control exercised over expenditure, including the reduction achieved in the percentage of GDP allocated to health services in the 1980s;

- the initiatives taken to manage clinical activity, especially in hospitals, centring on the role of clinic chiefs and the use of frame budgets.

The main weaknesses of the service are:

- lack of integration between primary care, hospital care and social services;

- a primary care system in which GPs do not act as gatekeepers and which results in a high proportion of direct referrals to hospital;

- a strong emphasis on institutional care which may not always be effective or efficient;

- limited choice for patients, although recent initiatives have begun to address this issue;

- the existence of waiting lists for some treatments;

- lack of incentives for efficiency, although again this is being tackled, especially in hospitals.

More generally, the idea of public competition offers an interesting parallel to the notion of managed competition as it has emerged recently in the NHS. By making patients the key determinants of where resources are allocated, the Swedish model indicates how the wishes of patients can be put first in the delivery of health care. Although this form of competition in action has so far been limited, its essential principles form the basis of a plausible alternative to reforms inspired by right-wing ideologies.

In conclusion, health services in Sweden exhibit many of the same problems that exist in the UK. The parallels are not exact, but the existence of waiting lists, the lack of incentives for efficiency, failures of coordination between sectors, and too heavy an investment in institutional care mirror widely-recognised weaknesses within the NHS. A high level of expenditure through tax funding enables certain problems to be overcome, such as the existence of outmoded buildings, but it does not of itself eliminate the need for rationing, nor does it ensure that services will be delivered in a way which is responsive to users.

Having long been considered a model of the advanced welfare state, Sweden is re-examinining its public services in an attempt to overcome the problems that exist. The outcome is uncertain, although the proposed shift of responsibility for non-acute care of the elderly from the county councils to municipal councils, the measures taken to extend consumer choice, the initiative to reduce waiting lists, and the interest shown in public competition indicate that the pattern of reform is likely to be incremental rather than radical. This is in keeping with the Swedish policy style, and it can be anticipated that public financing and provision of health care will continue to predominate. In comparison with the UK, the private sector remains very small, and there is little enthusiasm for extending its role on a significant scale.

The two areas in which Sweden contains lessons and pointers for other countries are public health policy and the management of clinical activity. In the case of public health, Sweden has a head start, with health statistics which are among the best in the world, and a commitment to social equity and comprehensive social welfare provision which has made an important contribution to the improvements in health that have occurred. The lead given by government in endorsing the Health for All by the Year 2000 strategy suggests that Sweden will continue to perform strongly in this area.

In the case of clinical activity, the appointment of clinical directors, the use of frame budgets, and the work undertaken by SPRI and the Council on Technology Assessment in Health Care illustrates the interest that exists in promoting the effective and efficient use of resources. These initiatives in part parallel developments in the UK, and in part they go beyond these developments, particularly in the work undertaken by the national agencies active in this field. In this sense, Swedish experience offers examples of policy instruments which might be tried elsewhere.

3 Holland

Holland has health services in which the public and private sectors both make significant contributions. Finance is raised mainly through incomes related social insurance contributions supplemented by private insurance premiums paid by higher income groups. Delivery is in the hands of private not-for-profit hospitals, and doctors are mainly private practitioners. Government regulations cover doctors' fees, hospital budgets, the use of health care technology and the provision of hospital beds. But day-to-day responsibility for the funding and provision of services rests with a range of predominantly private organisations and individuals.

These arrangements have enabled Holland to provide services of a high standard. Patients have a wide choice of providers and access to care is good. Expenditure is high in the international context and this is reflected in the comprehensive range of services available. However, the evidence suggests that resources are not always used efficiently, investment has tended to favour institutional services, and there have been difficulties in controlling expenditure on doctors' fees. There is also concern about the inequities that have arisen through the co-existence of social insurance and private insurance. A programme of reforms currently being implemented is designed to address these problems and to stimulate competition within the health services.

This chapter explores these issues by describing how health services are financed and provided. The predominance of hospital care is highlighted, and the absence of incentives for efficiency in hospitals is noted. The various measures taken to limit the use of health care technologies and to promote high quality care are then reviewed. Leading on from this, there is discussion of doctors' incomes and the management of clinical activity. This is followed by a summary of key health indicators and public health policy. The penultimate section of the chapter discusses the proposals for reform contained in the Dekker Report. Finally, the key strengths and weaknesses of health services in Holland are summarised.

Holland provides comprehensive health services to all of its population through a mixture of social insurance and private insurance. Health services expenditure comprised 8.5 per cent of GDP in 1987. 79 per cent of this expenditure came from public sources.

There are three main elements in the insurance arrangements. First, the whole population is covered by compulsory social insurance for serious and prolonged disability and sickness. Second, people earning below a certain income level (48,500 guilders or £15,700 in 1988) and those on social security are covered by social insurance for other health risks. Third, those above the income level take out private health insurance or pay for services directly. In 1988, around eight million people or 60 per cent of the population were included in the social insurance scheme and the remainder were covered by private insurance.

The social insurance scheme is administered by the sick funds. These are private not-for-profit organisations responsible for paying for health care for their members. There has been a gradual process of consolidation among the sick funds so that in many parts of the country there is only one fund in existence. Currently, there are about 45 sick funds in Holland. In view of the extent of government regulation, the sick funds in practice act as quasi-governmental institutions.

People in the social insurance scheme contribute a fixed percentage of their income, currently 4.8 per cent, and this is matched by employers. In addition, employers contribute to the compulsory insurance scheme for long-term sickness at the rate of 4.5 per cent of incomes. The contributions which individuals and employers make to the sick funds have to be approved by government. Family members are covered by these schemes. The package of benefits included in the social insurance scheme is determined nationally and individual sick funds have to guarantee access to necessary services for their members. Contributions are collected centrally and sick funds are reimbursed for expenditure incurred.

People who are privately insured can choose a policy from one of 70 competing insurers. The private insurance market has become increasingly competitive in recent years and a wide variety of packages is on offer including a range of coverage, co-payments and deductibles. Employees often receive a contribution from their employer to the costs of private insurance. Unlike the United States, most private insurance is taken out by individuals rather than companies or trade unions.

The co-existence of social insurance and private insurance is rooted in the historical development of health services in Holland. Proposals were formulated in 1975 to extend social insurance to the whole population, but these were not accepted. In part, this was because the government was seeking to limit public expenditure, and in part it resulted from political differences within the government on the extent to which social insurance provision should be expanded.

There is no evidence that people who are privately insured receive a better standard of care than the publicly insured, but certain inequities have arisen. For example, individuals who are just below the income level for entry into private insurance usually pay more for their insurance cover than individuals above the income level who are able to negotiate lower payments with private insurers. Furthermore, in the face of increasing competition, private insurers have become more careful in selecting risks. Premiums for elderly people and those in poor health have risen significantly while payments for younger, healthier members of the population have become more competitive. As Rutten and van der Werff (1982) have noted:

> there seems to be a continual divergence of the public and private sectors, the public for low-income earners being based on mutual solidarity, while the private insurance market tends to balance premium and risk (p. 190).

Recognition of these inequities was one of the factors behind the decision of the government to establish a review of health services financing and provision in 1986 (see below).

Most hospitals in Holland are run privately on a not-for-profit-basis. Historically, hospitals developed along religious lines, and each is managed by an independent board. Before 1983, hospitals were paid on the basis of costs actually incurred, and this tended to increase expenditure. Since 1983, prospective budgets have been used. These are negotiated between the purchasers of care (the sick funds and private insurers) and the providers. Budgets are based on a formula which currently has three components: population served, the number of beds and specialist services provided, and workload.

Doctors work mainly as private practitioners, although some are salaried employees. GPs are paid on a capitation basis for patients belonging to the social insurance scheme and a fee-for-service basis for private patients. Hospital consultants receive a fee-for-service and they are given a license to practise by the hospitals in which they work. A major concern in Holland has been the control of doctors' incomes and fees, and we discuss this further below.

There are nominal user charges for patients in the social insurance scheme. These cover hotel costs in the case of people with long-term illness, visits to specialists and prescribed drugs. Privately insured patients pay charges which depend on the extent of their cover. Some are fully reimbursed by the company with which they are insured, while others choose to accept large co-payments in return for lower premiums. Yet others have no insurance cover for some health services, for example primary care, and pay for these services out of pocket when required.

Expenditure Control

Expenditure on health services in Holland grew rapidly in the 1960s and 1970s but has stabilised at around 8.5 per cent of GDP in the 1980s. The government is unable to control overall expenditure directly and has to influence spending by various indirect means. Each year, for example, a public expenditure plan is issued setting out indicative targets for health services spending. This has no statutory force but is important in establishing the government's expectations on expenditure patterns. Other policy instruments include controls over the number of hospital beds and new hospital building; restrictions on the use of health care technology; fixed budgets for hospitals; and limits on doctors' fees. Government action on these issues has had some success but a number of outstanding problems remain. For example, the reduction in the number of hospital beds has been less than planned and doctors' incomes have not been controlled as effectively as the government has intended.

One of the most striking features of health care in Holland is the predominance of hospital services. Although there is a well-established primary care system in which GPs act as gatekeepers, there has also been a heavy investment in institutional care. In comparison, community health services and health promotion have received lower priority.

There are two main reasons for this. First, the funding of hospital services has been more securely based than that of community health services and health promotion. While hospitals are reimbursed mainly out of incomes related social insurance funds, community services are financed from government grants derived from general taxation. These grants have been more tightly constrained than social insurance. Furthermore, by paying for health services through social insurance, people in Holland consider that they have a right to treatment and they expect the services of GPs and hospitals to be available when required. This has added to the pressure for increased expenditure.

Second, until the introduction of prospective budgets in 1983, hospitals were reimbursed for the number of occupied bed days. This created an incentive to fill beds and helped to inflate hospital spending. It also worked against the development of day care and the substitution of inpatient care by outpatient services.

With a plentiful supply of beds and hospital specialists, patients have a wide choice of providers and there are no waiting lists (Rutten & van der Werff, 1982). On the other hand, there is some evidence to suggest that hospital resources may be used inefficiently. The number of inpatient days per capita is among the highest in the OECD countries, hospital stays are longer than average, and hospital expenditure per person and per admission are also high (OECD, 1987). As a number of analysts have argued, there would appear to be considerable scope for reducing hospital admissions and cutting lengths of stay (Enthoven, 1988; van de Ven, 1987).

To make this point is to highlight the absence of incentives for efficiency in Dutch hospitals. Sick funds are automatically reimbursed from the Central Insurance Fund for the expenditure incurred by their members and they have no incentives to limit hospital use. Also, sick funds are not able to contract selectively with providers but are required to pay for services from any hospital or doctor meeting certain quality requirements. As a consequence, the separation of funding and provision has not led to provider competition.

In the case of hospitals, prospective budgets create an incentive to keep expenditure within negotiated limits but beyond this there is little pressure to examine critically the use of resources. Furthermore, although hospital budgets are based in part on the number of patients treated, this forms such a small element in the overall budget (around 15-20 per cent) that there is only a weak incentive for hospitals to compete for patients. The introduction of prospective budgets for hospitals has helped to contain the growth of health services expenditure but has done little to promote greater efficiency within hospitals.

Technology Assessment and Quality Assurance

Another means of controlling expenditure concerns the use of health care technology. As Rutten and Banta (1988) have shown, Holland generally lies in the middle range of countries in the use of technologies such as CT scanners, open heart surgery and renal dialysis. Part of the reason for this is that government has statutory power to control the location of designated technologies by granting a license for the provision of services involving those technologies. Ten technologies are currently regulated in this way: renal dialysis, renal transplantation, radiotherapy, neurosurgery, cardiac surgery, heart catheterisation, nuclear medicine, CT scans, prenatal chromosome examination and neonatal intensive care.

The control exercised over these technologies is part of a broader interest in technology assessment. A government funded project has reviewed the future of health care technology and has provided an early warning of technologies likely to have a major impact on health services financing and provision. Also, the Health Council, an advisory body to government on scientific issues, publishes reports on a number of technologies, and is establishing an information clearing house on technology assessment. In addition, the Sick Funds Council, which oversees the work of the sick funds, has begun funding cost effectiveness analyses of technologies such as heart and liver transplants as a condition for payment (Rutten and Banta, 1988).

A related initiative has taken place in the field of quality assurance with the establishment in 1979 of the CBO (National Organisation for Quality Assurance in Hospitals). The CBO, which is independent and is supported financially by hospitals, has organised several consensus conferences and has taken the lead in developing standards and guidelines for use in health services. It also publishes an international newsletter on quality assurance and seeks to disseminate information about good practices. The CBO has taken a particular interest in medical audit and has stimulated the introduction of audit and peer review in both hospitals and primary care. The approach to audit in Holland is essentially voluntary but operates within a legal framework which places an obligation on health professionals to organise quality assurance activities.

Doctors' Incomes

One of the ways in which the government seeks to control expenditure is through limiting doctors' fees. The fee-for-service system for paying hospital consultants creates an incentive for consultants to treat more patients and thereby increase their incomes. To counteract this, a new system of remuneration has been introduced in stages since 1979. This system involves a sliding scale of fees in which the payment per patient falls as the number of patients treated exceeds specified limits. The fee schedule is based on a norm or target income for each specialty determined in national negotiations between the medical profession and the financers of health services, and approved by the government.

In practice, the system of 'regressive fees' as it is known in Holland has not succeeded in controlling doctors' incomes because it regulates price but not quantity. The available evidence indicates that doctors compensate for the reduction in fees by increasing their workload and are thus able to achieve the target income they set for themselves rather than that established by the government. This had led the government to take a tougher stance in its bargaining over incomes. National negotiations have become more acrimonious in recent years and doctors have gone on strike in protest at the strict controls which government has sought to introduce.

Unlike hospital doctors, GPs' incomes are based on capitation payments received from the social insurance scheme. This arrangement offers few incentives for GPs to use resources efficiently. Performance appears to be as variable as in the NHS. One recent experiment in Tilburg involved GPs participating in a budgetary system in which they received a bonus if their referrals to hospital consultants and physiotherapists were low, and if they reduced the number of prescriptions written. Both the experimental group of GPs and a control group achieved a considerable reduction in referral and prescribing rates, and the reduction in the experimental group was larger than that in the control.

More recently, a private insurance company has launched a HMO-type package and this is in the process of being evaluated. Plans for the future development of health services will provide a stronger incentive for further initiatives of this kind (see below). The interest shown in HMOs and in providing financial incentives for GPs are but two examples of a series of innovations concerned to achieve greater efficiency in the use of resources (Kirkman-Liff and van de Ven, 1989).

Managing Clinical Activity

Although most hospital consultants are private practitioners, they are usually required by the hospitals in which they work to play a full part in the management of the hospital and to engage in medical audit. However, like their counterparts in the UK, consultants remain independent practitioners and are not subject to the authority of other medical staff or non-medical managers. This is beginning to change following the introduction of prospective budgets for hospitals. As in Canada, there is a basic conflict between doctors who are paid by fee-for-service and hospital managers who have to keep within budgetary limits. Attempts to reconcile this conflict centre on improvements to hospital management, the participation of doctors in management, and the development of management training for doctors (Maarse, 1989).

In parallel, experiments are taking place with clinical budgets. In Maastricht, for example, medical staff work with managers to draw up a medical activity plan at the university hospital. This plan forms the basis of the hospital's budget and of departmental budgets. In the case of clinical services, doctors take on responsibility as budget holders. Similarly, at the university hospital in Utrecht, the management of services has been decentralised to clinical divisions led by physician managers. This parallels work underway in a number of countries including Canada, the UK and the US (Sunnybrook Report, 1988). As yet, however, initiatives of this kind have been limited to a small number of centres in Holland and in most hospitals medical staff have not been fully integrated into the management of services. Indeed, recent research has emphasised the independence of hospital consultants and the unwillingness of managers to challenge medical autonomy (Saltman and de Roo, 1989).

Health In Holland

Holland has an impressive health record with infant mortality rates and life expectancy both better than the OECD average. In the search for further improvements in health, Holland is committed to WHO's Health for All by the Year 2000 strategy. A report published by the Ministry of Welfare, Health and Cultural Affairs in 1986, *Health 2000*, set out the basis of the approach being followed. The report laid a heavy emphasis on personal behaviour and lifestyle as influences on health:

> Responsibility for health must rest first and foremost with the individual himself. In addition to rights (emancipation, independence, self determination) this also implies obligations (healthy conduct, responsible use of provision). (Ministry of Welfare, Health & Cultural Affairs, 1986, p. 4).

In the case of health services, the report argued that greater priority should be given to primary care and lower priority to hospital and specialist services:

> The referral pattern of general practitioner to specialist that has for so many years assured one way traffic towards secondary care must be broken (p. 5).

More responsibility should be assumed by GPs, district nurses and other primary care staff, and hospitals should be used only at a later stage. Outside the health services, the emphasis should be placed on intersectoral action, including a commitment to the WHO's Healthy Cities network.

The report highlighted the ageing of the population and its impact on the demand for health care. In 1980, Holland had a relatively low proportion of people aged over 65 among OECD countries, but this was projected to change significantly by 2030 (OECD, 1987). As the Ministry's report noted, this was likely to have significant implications in terms of the incidence of cancer, cardiovascular diseases, and other illnesses associated with ageing.

Unlike its Swedish counterpart, the report did not address the issue of social class inequalities in health and health services. The emphasis throughout was on the responsibility of individuals to look after themselves and to alter their lifestyles in order to improve health. This difference reflects the dominant value systems in the two countries, the Swedes attaching importance to collective provision and social solidarity, the Dutch giving higher priority to the rights and duties of individuals.

The Dekker Report

In 1986 the government established a committee chaired by Wisse Dekker, formerly managing director of the electronics group, Philips International, to review the structure and financing of health care. The stimulus behind the formation of the committee was threefold: concern about the limited effectiveness of government planning and regulation on health services; the lack of incentives for insurers and providers to use resources efficiently; and inequities in access to health care between different groups in the population. The committee was asked to conduct its work expeditiously and it duly reported in March 1987.

Underlying the committee's report was the view that a more market-oriented approach was desirable, involving competition between insurers and providers. This in turn implied a reduction in government regulation. To protect the position of more vulnerable groups in the population, the committee proposed a number of safeguards. These were designed to ensure the provision of basic health services to all while allowing individuals to top up their cover by purchasing additional insurance.

The Dekker committee's proposals involved two kinds of insurance: basic insurance covering essential health services, including visits to GPs and hospital consultants, hospital treatment, and some social services that were complementary to health services; and voluntary, supplementary insurance covering other services such as cosmetic surgery, adult dental care and abortion. The committee argued that basic insurance should be compulsory for everyone, the range of services should be determined by government, and insurers should be obliged to accept patients. Supplementary insurance would be optional and the services would be determined by the insurers. Again, though, insurers would be obliged to accept patients.

The scheme outlined by Dekker envisaged that the distinction between social insurance provided through the sick funds and private insurance provided through commercial companies should be removed. Both basic insurance and supplementary insurance would be available from a range of competing insurance organisations in the public and private sectors. In this way, patients covered under the existing social insurance arrangements would in future have a wider choice of insurers.

The cost of basic insurance would be met in two ways. First, employees and employers would continue to pay a uniform, fixed percentage of income into the Central Insurance Fund. Insurers would then receive a capitation payment from the Fund for each of their subscribers with the payment being based on actuarially adjusted risk. Second, individuals would pay a nominal premium representing a percentage of the cost of their cover directly to the insurance organisation. The size of the nominal premium, which was not specified by Dekker, would vary between insurers and this would stimulate competition on the demand side.

The effect of these proposals was to provide insurers with a fixed income. Unlike the sick funds, which were automatically reimbursed for expenditure incurred, insurers would have to take a much closer interest in the use made of services by their members. And having an obligation to accept patients, they would not be able to improve their performance through risk selection.

The other key element in the Dekker committee's proposals was that insurers should be able to contract selectively with providers. In practice, this would mean purchasing services for subscribers from those doctors and hospitals able to meet certain cost and quality requirements. The committee argued that selective contracting would stimulate competition between providers and would create powerful incentives for efficiency. Indeed, an important objective behind the Dekker report was to encourage the substitution of care outside hospital for inpatient treatment, and to promote the development of HMO-type organisations. In the longer term, this would involve a reduction in the number of hospital beds, the closure of inefficient hospitals, and a greater emphasis on primary care and health promotion.

One of the consequences of selective contracting by insurers anticipated by Dekker was a shift away from national determination of hospital budgets and doctors' fees to local negotiations. Thus, insurers would make contracts with one or more hospitals for the provision of specified services and would agree these contracts with the hospitals concerned. Equally, insurers would bargain directly with GPs and consultants to determine fees or salaries. From the government's point of view, this had the distinct advantage of making redundant the increasingly complex national pay negotiations with the medical profession.

Reaction to the Dekker report was mixed. Insurers expressed concern about the obligation to accept allcomers and at having their incomes largely fixed by government through payments from the Central Insurance Fund; doctors perceived a threat to their own position from the introduction of local pay bargaining and the enhanced role of insurers in negotiating service contracts; and there was uncertainty about the impact of competition on the quality of care. Also, despite the committee's attempt to ensure access to health care for all groups, doubts existed about whether this would be achieved in practice. As Lapre (1988) has stated:

> The main point of criticism is uncertainty as to whether the proposals offer sufficient guarantees to ensure that the weakest groups in society (lower income groups, old age pensioners, the handicapped) will in the future be able to realise their right to health care. The withdrawal of the government influence and the financial proposals that involve a larger proportion of the health care premiums and perhaps the cost of care being paid directly out of pocket, has led many people to fear that health care will be less financially accessible (p. 31).

Despite these misgivings, the Dekker report received a good deal of support, both from independent commentators such as Alain Enthoven (see Schut & van de Ven, 1987) and, more importantly, from the government itself. Following an extensive period of debate, the government announced that the report's proposals were to be implemented in stages, the first steps including the extension of compulsory social insurance to encompass a wider range of services, the introduction of a nominal premium alongside income related premiums, and the allocation to the sick funds of a fixed sum from the Central Insurance Fund. Major outstanding questions and concerns included how risk-related payments from the Central Insurance Fund to insurers would be calculated, the ability of insurers to negotiate contracts with providers, and the extent to which competition would occur when providers had a monopoly in certain areas.

From a UK perspective, the thinking behind the Dekker report is strikingly similar to the government's plans for the future of the NHS. Both sets of proposals seek to strengthen the position of the purchasers of care vis a vis the providers, and both aim to stimulate provider competition. A further similarity is the expectation that those responsible for finance or insurance will contract selectively with providers and will negotiate locally on issues such as the volume and cost of services to be provided and the reimbursement of doctors. At the same time, there is shared concern about the impact of competition on the quality of care and on the access to services of vulnerable groups. With managed competition the common objective, the balance to be struck between regulation and competition emerged as a major issue of debate in both countries.

Conclusion and Summary

Analysis of health services in Holland illustrates some of the issues which arise in a mixed economy of health. As we have seen, private finance contributes almost one quarter of health service expenditure, and private provision predominates. Government has few direct controls over the development of services but is able to influence decisions indirectly. The limited role played by the state (certainly compared with Sweden and the UK) and the provision of a safety net insurance system is a model which a number of contributors to the debate about the reform of the NHS have found attractive. As such, the evidence reviewed in this chapter should help to inform future discussion.

In summary, the major strengths of the Dutch system are:

- the provision of comprehensive services to the whole population;

- access to care is good and there are no waiting lists for treatment;

- overall expenditure has been brought under control in the 1980s and prospective budgets for hospitals have played an important part in this;

- patients have a wide choice between doctors and hospitals;

- government has acted to regulate the use of health care technology and to promote technology assessment;

- there is a strong interest in medical audit and quality assurance, led by the CBO.

The main weaknesses of the system are:

- financing arrangements have skewed investment toward hospital services and have made it difficult to substitute care outside hospitals for inpatient treatment;

- the available evidence suggests that hospital services are not always used efficiently;

- there is a lack of incentives for efficiency within hospitals;

- it has been difficult to control expenditure on doctors' incomes;

- there are adverse selection problems in the private insurance sector.

In conclusion, health services in Holland have avoided some of the problems that exist in the UK, but other weaknesses have also emerged. After a period in which more centralised government planning has been the main instrument used to tackle these weaknesses, the Dutch are now implementing reforms centred on the introduction of competition. These reforms are consistent with a tradition of pluralism and decentralisation, and they are of considerable interest because of their similarity with the Thatcher Government's proposals for reforming the NHS.

Despite significant differences between health services financing and provision in the UK and Holland, there is a convergence of thinking around the idea of managed competition as a strategy for reform. It would seem that the reasons for this include the influence of Alain Enthoven, whose support for competition has attracted extensive interest in both countries; recognition that government planning and global budgets may be effective tools for limiting overall expenditure but by themselves are insufficient in providing incentives for efficiency; and a willingness to draw on ideas and expertise from business management in designing plans for the reform of health services.

4   West Germany

West Germany, like Holland, relies on a mixture of public and private finance and provision. The role of government is limited to providing the legislative and regulatory framework within which services are delivered. Self-government by the sick funds, medical associations, hospital managers, and private insurers is heavily emphasised, and markets co-exist with planning in a mixed economy of health care.

The bulk of health services in West Germany are financed through a social insurance scheme. This has been developed to the point where comprehensive health care is provided to the vast majority of the population. Health services are generously funded and there is a plentiful supply of doctors and hospital beds.

A major concern in recent years has been the increasing cost of health care. Government has pursued a programme of reforms designed to contain expenditure and to achieve stability in contribution rates to the social insurance scheme. These reforms include the establishment of a national forum to develop guidelines on spending, prospective budgets for hospitals, controls over drugs expenditure, and the extension of user charges.

This chapter explores these issues by describing how health services are financed and provided. The instruments used to limit expenditure are reviewed, and the programme of reforms is outlined. The difficulty of achieving significant change in the German political system is emphasised. Finally, the key strengths and weaknesses of health services are summarised.

Health Services Finance

West Germany provides comprehensive health services to its population through a mixture of private insurance and social insurance. Health services expenditure comprised 8.2 per cent of GDP in 1987 (Schieber and Poullier, 1989). 78 per cent of this expenditure came from public sources. After growing rapidly in the 1970s, health service expenditure as a proportion of national income has broadly stabilised in recent years.

There are two main elements in the insurance arrangements. First, there is a compulsory social insurance scheme for people earning below a certain income level (55,000 DM or £20,000 in 1988) and those on social security. Second, those above the income level may opt out of the scheme and take out private insurance providing equivalent cover. In practice, around 90 per cent of the population are members of the social insurance scheme, and most of the remainder subscribe to private insurance.

As in Holland, social insurance is administered by the sick funds. These are private, not-for-profit organisations responsible for paying for the health care of their members. Currently, there are about 1200 sick funds. Membership of funds is usually based on people's employment or area of residence. Each fund manages its own affairs and representatives of trade unions and employers play a major part in this process.

People in the social insurance scheme contribute a fixed percentage of their income and this is matched by employers. Family members are included within these arrangements. In 1987 employees and employers each contributed an average of 6.4 per cent of income to the scheme. However, there is considerable variation in contributions around this average, amounting to a two-fold difference at the extremes. This reflects the different risk structures and income levels within the funds. As we discuss later, a key issue for the future is how to equalise the incomes of the sick funds in order to reduce variations in contribution rates.

The basic package of benefits included in the social insurance scheme is determined nationally. A comprehensive range of services is available encompassing all forms of medical and dental care. As Beske (1988) has noted, social insurance provision has been expanded over the years to the point 'where virtually everything possible in medicine is granted to members of the statutory system' (p. 104).

People who are privately insured can choose a policy from one of 40 competing insurers. Premiums are determined by the age of the insured person on entry and are paid jointly by employees and employers. Insurers are not allowed to increase premiums for members who develop a serious illness after entry. This helps to ensure continuity of membership. The attractions of opting out for many of those on high incomes are that private insurance is cheaper than social insurance, and it may also offer cover for additional services. There is no evidence that the standard of care for private patients is higher than that received by sick fund patients.

In addition to the resources for health care which derive from insurance contributions, some finance is provided through general taxation and direct patient payments. Currently, patients pay a small charge towards the cost of prescribed drugs, spectacles and aids. Dental check-ups are free, but dental treatment and the provision of dentures involve payments averaging 50 per cent of the cost. There is also a daily charge of 5 DM (£1.80) for inpatient hospital care and for rehabilitation, up to a maximum of 14 days.

Recent health reforms have extended user charges and the details are discussed later in the chapter. Partly as a consequence of these reforms, there has been an increase in the number of people taking out private insurance to supplement the cover provided by social insurance. Typically, supplementary private insurance covers dental treatment, hospital amenities and services not included in the social insurance scheme, such as nursing homes.

Health Service Provision

There is a mixed pattern of hospital ownership. Public hospitals operate alongside private hospitals, both for profit and not-for-profit. The income of hospitals is based on daily rate charges paid by the sick funds and private insurers. These charges are determined prospectively in negotiations between hospital managers and the purchasers of care. Capital investment is financed separately by the state governments for those hospitals included in the state hospital plan.

Hospital doctors are salaried employees, while doctors working out of hospital are private practitioners paid on a fee-for-service basis. There is little overlap between the two and one of the features of health services in West Germany is the extent to which specialist outpatient care is provided away from hospital. Approximately half of the doctors working in the community are specialists and half are general practitioners. Liaison between hospitals and GPs is often poor, and the absence of hospital outpatient services limits the effective provision of health care.

Fee-for-service reimbursement has encouraged specialist doctors to expand the range of services they provide in the community. As a consequence, extensive use is made of diagnostic tests, there is an incentive for doctors to acquire new technology to increase the services they are able to offer, and there is unnecessary duplication of services between hospitals and the community (Schulenburg, 1983). For these and other reasons, expenditure on health services has increased rapidly and has prompted action by government to control costs (see below).

The high level of spending on health services and the comprehensive nature of the social insurance scheme means that there is no shortage of hospitals and doctors. Patients have a wide choice of providers and waiting lists are non-existent. Indeed, in many ways, health services in West Germany are a mirror image of the NHS with over-provision and high spending being perceived as the major challenges facing policy makers.

Of particular concern is the over-supply of doctors. In an attempt to tackle this problem, there has been an extension of the training period required of doctors before they enter practice, and moves to reduce the intake of students to medical schools. These measures have had limited impact, despite agreement between government and the federal medical associations on the need for action. The main reason is that state governments control medical education and their priorities often differ from those of federal government. Also, a court ruling of 1961 makes it unconstitutional to limit the number of doctors in practice. Although powers have been introduced to prevent doctors from setting up practice in over-doctored areas, this affects only the distribution of doctors and not the total number in work (Webber, 1988).

Expenditure Control

Cost containment has been the main driving force behind health care reforms in the 1970s and 1980s. Social insurance contributions rose from 8 per cent of income in 1970 to nearly 13 per cent in 1987. The employer's share of contributions has been an important factor in increasing industrial costs and has led employers to put pressure on government to limit the burden imposed by the social insurance scheme.

Hospitals

Efforts to control hospital costs centre on negotiations between the purchasers of care and hospital managers. The sick funds and private insurers whose members account for more than 5 per cent of the hospital's inpatient days form a 'common office' to negotiate with the hospital (Glaser, 1987). Each side makes use of data on the comparative cost of different hospitals and agree a daily rate for the coming year. The rate is intended to reflect that paid to efficient hospitals.

In practice, these arrangements provide no incentives for efficiency. The effect of daily rate charges, paid irrespective of the intensity of care, is to encourage long hospital stays. This is because the expense of the early part of treatment can be subsidised by the later stages of care, when the costs of the patient's stay are lower. Daily rate charges also provide an incentive to hospitals to keep their beds full rather than to promote early discharge.

In recognition of these weaknesses, the law was changed in 1984 to strengthen incentives for efficiency in hospitals (Altenstetter, 1986). The new arrangements involve the use of prospective budgets for hospitals based on anticipated utilisation rates. If actual utilisation differs from that planned, then the budget is adjusted accordingly.

Adjustments are made on the basis that hospitals may retain 25 per cent of the additional income they earn if utilisation is higher than expected. Equally, hospitals are required to carry 25 per cent of the losses if utilisation is lower than expected. This formula reflects the ratio of fixed to variable costs (75:25) in German hospitals. Budgetary adjustments are not made for specialised services which are excluded from the basic hospital budget.

The effectiveness of these reforms as an instrument for containing costs in the hospital sector has been questioned by a number of commentators (see, for example, Altenstetter, 1987). As a consequence, there is increasing interest in the use of DRG-based reimbursement for hospitals. To date, however, DRGs have been the subject of debate only, and there has been no experience of their application in practice. Indeed, state governments have expressed strong objections to their introduction.

Nevertheless, if lengths of stay continue to be high by international standards, future reforms cannot ignore the perverse incentive created by existing methods of reimbursement. Currently, there is much interest in strengthening the position of purchasers of care in their relations with hospitals. This includes requiring hospitals to publish lists of their prices as a way of creating greater transparency and encouraging the use of lower cost hospitals. Also, sick funds are now able to cancel contracts with hospitals which they consider to be inefficient or too expensive.

However, the use of this power is limited because state governments, which provide the resources for capital developments, have to give their approval before contracts are cancelled. They are often reluctant to do this because of concern about public reaction to reductions or closure of hospital services. A further complication is that hospitals are usually financed by several sick funds and individual funds are unwilling to move out of step with others because the choices of their members would be reduced. In this sense, competition between the funds for members inhibits their ability to act as prudent purchasers.

Doctors' Fees and The Review of Clinical Practices

Rather more success has been achieved in controlling expenditure on doctors'fees. The key instrument here is the global budget for fees negotiated annually between the medical associations and the association of sick funds. Once the budget is agreed, it is left to the medical associations to pay doctors according to the number and type of services provided.

Payments are based on a fee schedule agreed at the federal level. The monetary value of each service varies with the quantity of services delivered. As Schulenburg (1983) has noted:

if the claims of all physicians and those of all dentists, respectively, exceed the prearranged cap, all fees will be reduced proportionately (p. 335).

The structure of the fee schedule is the subject of continuing negotiation. In the past there has been concern that diagnostic tests were over-valued in comparison with direct medical treatment. Changes introduced in 1987 have sought to correct these biases and even out the distribution of income both between GPs and specialists. As a consequence of these changes, the budget for fees is divided into different blocks, and this is intended to avoid additional spending on tests taking money away from fees for consultations and other services. More recently, debate has centred on the replacement of fee-for-service reimbursement by capitation payments, although this is being resisted by the medical associations.

The payment claims of doctors working out of hospital are routinely analysed by the regional medical associations. Doctors whose practices deviate significantly from the mean (usually 40 per cent) are called to account before a review board. Sanctions include counselling and advice, warnings and fines. The evidence suggests that 10 per cent of doctors are reviewed in this way, but only in a few cases are financial penalties invoked (Dohler, 1987). Doctors are usually able to tailor their practices to maximise income without being called to account. As Dohler has observed:

> reviewing physicians' efficiency in the Federal Republic of Germany
> is more an instrument of maintaining the status quo of well worn
> practice patterns than an instrument of effective control (p. 20).

Recent changes provide two other means of reviewing clinical practices. First, the sick funds and medical associations have been given the power to investigate random samples of 2 per cent of doctors working out of hospital each quarter. The aim is not simply to examine claims for payment, but also to undertake medical audit in order to promote higher standards of care. Consistent with the principle of self-government, federal government has laid down a requirement for medical audit in legislation and has given responsibility to the sick funds and medical associations to determine how this should be done.

Second, the long-established 'control doctor' system, whose main role has been to avoid malingering by patients, has been reorganised. In future, control doctors will provide a medical advisory service to the sick funds and will monitor the necessity of medical care in relation to home care, rehabilitation, orthodontics and other services. However, the doctors who are employed for these purposes usually have limited qualifications and are not well placed to challenge the decisions of their peers (Jost, 1990).

A specific initiative designed to control costs and promote greater efficiency was taken in Bavaria in 1979. The so-called Bavarian Contract emerged out of negotiations between the regional medical association and association of sick funds with the aim of encouraging doctors to provide as much care as possible in the community and to reduce hospital admissions. Financial incentives built into the contract provided extra resources for doctors working in the community if expenditure in other areas declined.

As Altenstetter (1987) and Bally (1982) have noted, the evidence on the operation of the Bavarian Contract is not conclusive. It would seem that the incentives facing individual doctors were not strong enough to change patterns of medical practice significantly. Furthermore, the contract presupposed the existence of alternative services and forms of support in the community, and these were not always available.

Health Reforms

Concern on the part of federal government at increasing costs has resulted in a number of reforms. Of particular importance was the establishment by law in 1977 of Concerted Action, a national conference of 60 participants from all major sectors of health care. The conference meets twice a year and recommends growth rates for different types of expenditure. The aim is to link increases in expenditure to movements in wages and the tax base. Much of the work of Concerted Action is based on advice and reports prepared by a committee of seven medical and economics experts. This committee meets monthly and it develops proposals for debate on key issues.

The recommendations of Concerted Action have no statutory force. Rather, they serve as guidelines for negotiations between the funders and providers of care. Concerted Action has become the major forum in which the main participants in health care meet in public to decide upon future developments. Although it has had some success in moderating the rate of increase in expenditure, new pressures have emerged during the 1980s leading to further measures on the part of the government.

The most recent health reform legislation was enacted in 1988 and came into operation in 1989. The principal aim of the legislation is to achieve stability in the rate of social insurance contributions. This is to be pursued mainly by control over expenditure on drugs, increases in user charges and changes to the services included within the social insurance scheme.

The steps taken to control expenditure on drugs reinforce earlier moves to limit expenditure in this area. OECD data show that in 1983 19 per cent of the health care budget was spent on drugs compared with 10 per cent for OECD countries as a whole (OECD, 1987). Attempts to control expenditure on drugs have included publication of a negative list of drugs, normally used in the treatment of minor illnesses, which are not covered by the sick funds; and the establishment of a Transparency Commission which publishes information on the price of drugs.

The 1988 reforms go further by establishing 'reference prices' for drugs with generic substitutes. The sick funds will pay this price in full if generic drugs are prescribed. On the other hand, if the patient or doctor chooses to use a more expensive drug instead of the generic equivalent then the patient has to pay the difference in price. Linked to this change, the law requires sick funds and medical associations to introduce prospective drugs budgets for doctors. Precisely how this will be done is the subject of continuing negotiation, but the aim is to introduce controls over the volume of prescribing as well as prices.

Increases in patient payments affect a range of services. The prescription charges for drugs not covered by reference prices has been increased from 2 to 3 DM (70p to £1.10). From 1992 patients will pay 15 per cent of the cost of these drugs instead of a flat rate charge, up to a maximum of 15 DM (£5.50). In the case of dental treatment, patients pay between 40 per cent and 60 per cent of the cost of the treatment. The lower figure applies to those who attend their dentist regularly. Also, for the first time, patients will pay the full cost of dental treatment and will be reimbursed by the sick funds for the amount for which the fund is responsible.

Daily charges for hospital stays and rehabilitation have been increased, and from 1991 will be set at 10 DM (£3.60) per day. At the same time, patients who do not use health services other than for normal health checks during the course of a year will be eligible for a 'no claims bonus' of one month's contribution to the social insurance scheme. These changes are all intended to make patients more aware of the cost of treatment and to reduce unnecessary demand for services.

The other major reform concerns the range of services included in the social insurance package. In a number of cases, this involves a reduction in services, as in the payment of taxi fares to hospital for patients unable to travel without assistance. In other cases, extra benefits have been added, the most important of which is home care for severely disabled people. Also, special payments are to be made to doctors for carrying out regular health checks on the over-35s. These payments are in addition to the global budget for doctors' fees and are intended to provide an incentive to doctors to give higher priority to preventive work.

As this assessment indicates, the health reform programme has had the most impact on patients and the pharmaceutical companies. Doctors have been affected by the moves discussed earlier to review clinical practices more rigorously, but as these are based on peer review and will be implemented under the aegis of the medical associations, they have provoked little controversy. Similarly, the position of hospitals remains largely unchanged even though government has sought to develop instruments to encourage sick funds to cancel contracts with inefficient hospitals. The sick funds themselves have been put under financial pressure through the policy of contribution rate stability, but with the economy growing and contributions buoyant, this has yet to have a major impact.

For the longer term, a wide range of reforms are under discussion (Henke, 1989), and there is continuing discussion about how the weaknesses of the present system can be tackled through incremental changes. A key issue here is the future role of the sick funds. As we noted earlier, contribution rates to the funds vary significantly and there is concern at the inequities this entails. Various proposals for achieving equalisation have been put forward, but as yet there is no agreed solution. One possibility is to establish a single national fund, but this is not considered to be politically feasible.

A related concern is consumer choice between sick funds. At present, white collar workers have greater choice than blue collar workers in that they may join the so-called 'substitute funds', whereas blue collar workers have to join the company fund, where this exists, or the local fund. The debate on the most recent health reforms included demands to give all those in the social insurance scheme the freedom to choose the fund they wanted to join. Opposition from the white collar funds, which were concerned at the prospect of manual workers applying for membership and changing their risk structure, was successful in deferring resolution of this issue to a later date (Webber, 1988).

A more general point follows from this, namely the difficulty of achieving change within the West German political system. Not only are there powerful interests within the health service, but also government is itself relatively weak. This applies both at the federal level, where coalition government tends to result in compromises between the political parties, and in the balance of power between federal and state governments. The latter play an important part in the health services and they do not always pursue the same goals as federal government.

As a consequence, minor adjustments to the status quo are the limit of what is possible and the reforms which do emerge are not always internally consistent. This is illustrated by the 1988 legislation which introduced an extension to the social insurance scheme as part of a package designed to contain costs and increase charges. The reason for this was the wish of the Minister concerned to show that cost containment was not the only goal and that government was committed to the social insurance scheme. Unless the political system itself changes, future reforms are likely to follow a similar pattern.

Conclusion and Summary

Health services in West Germany have developed rapidly in the post-war period and now provide comprehensive cover to the population. Yet as the health reform programme illustrates, there is continuing concern at the cost of health care, and government has been forced to act to limit the increase in expenditure. As a consequence, patients will pay more for the use of some services, and drugs companies will be squeezed by the introduction of reference prices. It remains to be seen whether these and other reforms will be sufficient to bring about stability in social insurance contributions.

In summary, the main strengths of the West German system are:

- the provision of comprehensive services to the whole population;

- access to care is excellent and there are no waiting lists for treatment;

- patients have a wide choice of doctors and hospitals;

- overall expenditure has been brought under control in the 1980s through various cost-containment measures.

The main weaknesses of the system are:

- hospital services are characterised by inefficiencies, including a surplus of beds and long hospital stays. Reimbursement of hospitals through daily rate charges has contributed to this;

- fee-for-service reimbursement of doctors outside hospital creates an incentive for the excessive supply of services even though overall expenditure on fees is subject to a budgetary cap;

- there is an over-supply of doctors;

- there is lack of integration between hospital and non-hospital care and duplication of services between the two;

- there is high expenditure on drugs, despite moves to limit this expenditure;

- there are inequities in the social insurance scheme in that contribution rates to the sick funds vary widely even though the range of services is basically the same.

It is also worth noting that health in West Germany is close to the OECD average as judged by indicators such as perinatal and infant mortality and life expectancy. In this respect, West Germany lags behind countries such as Sweden, Holland and Canada, and is in a similar position to the UK. Public health policy has been relatively neglected, with the reform of health services taking precedence over other issues in the health field.

In conclusion, health services in West Germany perform well by some criteria and poorly by others. If over-provision and inefficiencies persist on the supply side, government will be faced with the choice of sanctioning increases in contribution rates, strengthening the hands of the sick funds as purchasers, increasing user charges still further, or reducing the scope of the social insurance scheme. In view of the importance of contribution rate stability as a plank of current policy, it is unlikely that increases in rates will be permitted in the near future. Equally, the opposition of state governments to tighter controls over hospital finances probably rules out action by the sick funds over budgets. The most plausible scenario is, therefore, a continuation of the 1988 reforms with patients paying more in direct charges and the range of services available being reduced. If this does indeed happen, an increasing number of people are likely to choose private insurance instead of social insurance, and West Germany will move closer to Holland in terms of the proportion of the population covered by the two sectors.

The areas in which West Germany contains lessons and pointers for other countries mainly concern doctors' fees and the review of clinical practices. The acceptance of a cap on fees by the medical associations, and the role of the associations in distributing the budget to their members, indicates the direction in which Holland and Canada might move. Similarly, the new arrangements for medical audit, involving the medical associations and sick funds reviewing the practices of a random sample of doctors working out of hospital, parallel developments in the UK. Much the same applies to the introduction of prospective drugs budgets for GPs and the use of special incentive payments to encourage doctors to carry out health checks on patients. Perhaps most important of all, the Bavarian Contract, although not wholly successful, foreshadows GP budgets, and indicates that the design of budgets needs to be handled carefully if clinical practices are to be changed in the desired direction.

5 United States

The US health care system is a paradox of excess and deprivation. This is the view of the eminent health care expert, Alain Enthoven, whose ideas have been so influential in shaping the UK government's views about reform of the NHS (Enthoven and Kronick, 1989).

On the one hand, the United States spends more on health care than any other country. In 1987 spending amounted to over $500 billion (£300 billion) for a population of approximately 250 million people, or $2,000 (£1,200) per person. This accounted for over 11 per cent of GDP. In comparison with the UK, the average American incurs nearly three times the level of health expenditure and has almost double the proportion of her national income devoted to it.

In the midst of this affluence, however, there is serious deprivation. Over 30 million Americans have no financial protection against the expenses of medical care — they have no insurance cover, either public or private. Millions more have only limited coverage that leaves them vulnerable to enormous financial risks. And uncounted millions have coverage that excludes pre-existing medical conditions.

How has the co-existence of excess and deprivation come about? And what are the policy responses that have been directed towards it? These are the questions addressed in this chapter. It starts with a description of the main components of the US finance and delivery system. This is followed by an account of policies designed to restrain spiralling health care costs. The chapter describes the shift of emphasis from regulation to market competition — as a means of cost control — and goes on to look at the emergence of a new form of price regulation operated through federal government payments of the health care costs of the elderly. Next, the degree of consumer choice is considered. And finally, the limited access to health care facilities suffered by some groups are examined together with current proposals for overcoming this problem.

The Financing and Provision of Services

Most health care in the US is provided by doctors and hospitals in the private sector. In 1987, for example, of the approximately 5,600 short-term general hospitals, nearly three-quarters were owned privately: 58 per cent were private not-for-profit organisations, while 15 per cent were investor-owned, for-profit hospitals. The remaining 27 per cent of hospitals were state or local government owned and operated on a not-for-profit basis. The concentration of provision within the private sector was even more marked in terms of the distribution of hospital beds, with over 80 per cent in privately owned hospitals (American Hospitals Association, 1988).

Within the private sector, there has been a reduction in the numbers of not-for-profit hospitals and beds during the 1980s, while the for-profit sector has expanded. The size of these changes has not, however, been sufficient to affect the dominance of the not-for-profit sector: there are still seven beds in not-for-profit hospitals for every one in a for-profit hospital.

While the private sector, whether for-profit or not-for-profit, dominates health care provision, sources of finance are more mixed. These fall into four main categories:

- direct patient payments;

- private insurance;

- the federally funded Medicare programme for the elderly and certain disabled groups;

- federal/state funded Medicaid programmes for low income families.

Direct patient payments

Most doctors and hospitals operate on a fee-for-service basis. Patients are charged for services at the time of use. The majority of the population have the risk of incurring sudden and unexpected bills reduced through insurance arrangements which are either privately or publicly funded. However, an estimated 37 million people have no insurance. In addition, many people are under insured. Others choose or are required to pay part of their bills directly under the terms of their insurance contracts.

As a result of all these factors, in 1987, just under 28 per cent of personal health expenditure was financed through direct patient payments. The proportion of any bill that is covered in this way varies quite widely among different categories of health spending. Less than 10 per cent of hospital care is paid for directly while about one quarter of doctors' fees and three quarters of the drugs bill are paid in this way.

Private Health Insurance

Approximately two-thirds of the population have some form of private health insurance (Raffel and Raffel, 1989), although it accounts for only about one-third of total health expenditure. For most people, insurance is taken out through an employer under a 'group' policy or enrollment. The generally lower risk status of people in employment, and certain economies of scale, mean that group policies usually cost less and offer a broader range of benefits than individual plans.

Policies are offered by two main types of insurer. The longest established insurers are the Blue Cross/Blue Shield plans which developed during the 1930s and 1940s. The initial impetus came from the Blue Cross Hospital Expense Insurance Plan which grew rapidly during the 1930s. This was followed by the Blue Shield Insurance Plans covering the cost of doctors' services which grew up in the 1940s. The 'Blues' were established under special state laws and supervised by state insurance departments. Today there are over 60 Blue Cross/Blue Shield plans covering 50 states. Although formally independent, they have co-operating agreements which permit the transfer of enrollment from one plan to another (when a person moves between states) without any waiting period or loss of continuity.

Since the early 1970s, the Blues have started to lose market share as cheaper commercial insurance companies have entered the market. Companies such as Prudential and Equitable now cover over half of the privately insured population, generally through employer-based group policies.

Private insurance reduces the risk of financial difficulty arising through illness but it does not eliminate it. Most insurance policies have benefit ceilings that are not sufficient to cover serious, long-term illness. To allow for this contingency, many people supplement their normal health insurance with major medical expense — or catastrophic illness — insurance. These policies have grown rapidly since they were introduced in the 1950s. Typically they cover 80 per cent of the costs of catastrophic illness up to a specified ceiling. In 1980, for example, three-quarters of those with catastrophic insurance had a benefit ceiling of $250,000 (£150,000). Thereafter the person is thrown upon his or her own resources, those of the state or city government, or charity.

The prevalence of employment based insurance means that health benefits are now a standard perk of the job for most Americans. As such, employers have found it difficult to contain their cost. A 1983 survey of the Fortune 500 industrial companies and the 250 largest non-industrial companies found that health benefits accounted for nearly one quarter of their after tax profits. Put rather differently, in 1984 it was estimated that health benefits added about 10 per cent to the price of a cheaper model of car produced by the Chrysler Corporation (Green, 1986). According to some economists this is becoming a major issue governing the international competitiveness of US industry.

One response to rising costs has been a tendency for most large employers to move towards self insurance. Under this arrangement, they purchase administrative services from conventional insurance companies but pay for the care directly out of their operating budgets. This provides them with more direct control over costs than can usually be achieved through third party payments. In 1988, over half of employees with company sponsored insurance were covered by some type of self-insurance plan.

Another approach to escalating costs, adopted in recent years, has been to try to make people covered by private insurance more sensitive to the actual costs of using health services. One way has been through the introduction of cost sharing. This takes two main forms. It may be applied to insurance premiums so that people are required to bear a proportion of the cost alongside government or employer contributions. In this case it is designed to encourage consumers to be more discriminating about the range of benefits they select when choosing between competing plans. Alternatively, cost sharing can be applied at the time of use through co-payments, deductibles or payments for services not covered by insurance plans. All of these mechanisms are designed to make consumers more aware of the cost of services and to deter overuse.

The Medicare Programme

Medicare is a federal health insurance programme for people of 65 years and over. It also covers certain disabled groups, especially those requiring dialysis treatment for kidney disease. The programme was introduced in 1965 in an effort to ensure access to health services for the elderly population at a stage in their lives when the combined effects of higher risks of illness and reduced incomes made it difficult for them to meet private insurance premiums. At present, Medicare accounts for about 20 per cent of total health expenditure.

The programme has two parts. *Hospital insurance* (known as "Part A") helps to pay for inpatient hospital care, some nursing home care, home health care and hospice care. *Medical insurance* (known as "Part B") contributes towards the costs of doctors' fees and other non inpatient services. Both parts of the programme, however, require patients to bear a portion of their costs. From a UK perspective these cost sharing arrangements appear to represent quite a substantial burden (see Table 1 overleaf).

In 1987, Medicare patients were responsible for personal payments amounting to nearly 23 per cent of the total costs of acute inpatient care.

Table 1   Cost Sharing under Medicare

SERVICE		CHARGE TO PATIENT	
Acute hospital inpatient stay* (not including doctors' fees)	0 - 60 days	up to	$540
	61 - 90 days	above + $135 per day	
	91 - 150 days**	above + $270 per day	
Doctors' fees:		$75	+ 20 percent of additional approved charges
			+ Full cost of difference between actual and approved charges
Outpatient Acute Hospital Services		As doctors' fees	
Blood Transfusions		Full cost of first three pints	
Psychiatric Hospital Care		Full cost after 190 days per lifetime	
Hospice Care		Full cost after two 90 day and one 30 day period	

Source: US Department of Health and Human Resources, 1988.

* These entitlements refer to a benefit period: a benefit period ends when an individual has been out of hospital for 60 consecutive days. There is no limit to the number of benefit periods an individual may have.

** These 60 days are known as reserve days and an individual is entitled to only 60 reserve days per lifetime.

Because of these liabilities nearly three quarters of Medicare beneficiaries subscribe to supplementary private insurance schemes known as medi-gap policies. However, this leaves a quarter of the elderly population without any supplementary insurance and, as one recent study showed, these tend to be poorer families. Only 44 per cent of families with incomes of less than $5,000 (£3,000) per year had a medigap policy compared with 87 per cent of those families with incomes of $25,000 (£15,000) or more per year. Moreover, those families reporting poor states of health were also less likely to have a medigap policy than those reporting good health (Christensen et al., 1987).

It is also important to point out that Medicare insurance is not compre-hensive. Table 2 indicates some of the major services that are excluded. Among those listed, the costs of nursing home care — other than short post-hospital stays — and prescription drugs were the most important. In 1987 it was estimated that expenditure on these items amounted to nearly 40 per cent of the total Medicare budget.

Table 2   Services not covered by Medicare

Dental care	Immunisations except pneumococcal and hepatitis B vaccinations or immunisations required because of any injury or immediate risk of infection
Drugs and medicines prescribed by doctors or self administered	
Eye examinations and glasses	Long term care (nursing homes)
Routine foot care	Nursing care on a full time basis at home
Hearing examinations and hearing aids	
Injections which can be self administered, e.g. insulin	

Medicaid

The Medicaid Programme — which like Medicare was introduced in 1965 — is designed to reduce financial barriers to health care for certain low income groups. Finance is provided jointly by the state and federal governments and, in 1987, amounted to just over 11 per cent of total personal health care expenditure.

The programme is administered independently by individual states within broad federal guidelines. Receipt of Medicaid benefits is usually linked to the welfare system (which is comparable in principle to the UK income support system) and covers the health care costs of low income people who are elderly, blind, disabled or members of families with dependent children. It does not, however, offer protection to all low income groups. Those who are not eligible for assistance include non-elderly single people, most two-parent families, and families with a father working at a low-paid job. One third of children living below the poverty line have no insurance coverage. Moreover, individual states have a degree of flexibility in setting income eligibility levels, in the range of services covered and the duration of coverage. As a result there are considerable variations between the way individuals in identical circumstances are treated in different states. California, for example, has one of the most generous schemes whereas Mississippi applies far more stringent rules.

Those people who fall outside the Medicaid safety net are not denied all access to care. Other sources of finance for the uninsured include: various local and state government contributions to public hospitals; private hospitals who have traditionally cross-subsidised the costs of some patients who are unable to meet their bills from the charges levied on paying patients; federal government funds targetted at specific groups such as veterans of the armed forces; and charitable contributions from individuals, corporations and private foundations.

Managed Care

The disenchantment felt by many people at the escalating costs of traditional forms of health finance has led to a growth in demand for alternative methods of finance and delivery which aim to offer high quality care while controlling costs. Collectively these have become known as managed care systems. Health maintenance organisations (HMOs) were the first of these alternatives to develop.

In the traditional insurance-based system, financial risk is borne by an insurance company which pays the doctor and/or hospital on a fee-for-service basis. This gives the doctor no incentive to minimise costs. Quite the reverse: there is a financial incentive to overtreat through the provision of unnecessary services. HMOs seek to counteract these tendencies.

A typical HMO operates on a pre-paid or prospective payment basis. Patients enrol through the payment of a set annual fee, usually through their employer. In return the HMO contracts to provide all the health care that is deemed necessary. This may be delivered through a staff model HMO in which doctors are employed directly on a salaried basis. Alternatively the HMO — acting as an insurer — may contract with a large group practice to provide care (a group model), or with a number of practices (a network model), or with a number of solo practitioners or small groups (an independent practice association (IPA)) (Stoline and Weiner, 1988).

In many HMOs doctors are either salaried or paid a set fee per enrollee instead of receiving a fee-for-service. This removes the incentive to over-utilise hospital services and provides an incentive for them to be cost conscious by minimising those treatments which produce few, if any, benefits. Even in those HMOs which operate on a fee-for-service basis, utilisation controls, such as pre-hospital admission certification and other methods of managing care, are an essential component of a strategy designed to contain costs.

The growth of HMOs over the last twenty years has been dramatic. In 1970 there were fewer than 30 serving just under 3 million people. By 1980 their number had grown to 230 serving 9 million people, and by 1988 there were over 700 catering for over 29 million people (Stoline and Weiner, 1988). In fact, growth during the 1980s was probably too rapid. As a result, many HMOs have experienced financial problems. In 1986 nearly three quarters of them made losses. The increase in price competition which HMOs did much to precipitate, tighter federal government limits on payments through the Medicare system (see below), and poor financial management have all contributed towards these losses. After a degree of shake-out growth is now proceeding more slowly.

With the slowing down in the spread of HMOs, a modified form of insurance-based, fee-for-service health finance has grown in popularity. This is offered through preferred provider organisations (PPOs). In essence, these are insurance plans which are able to offer lower premiums to enrolees because they negotiate fee-for-service discounts with specified doctors and hospitals in return for guaranteeing them a given volume of work. Part of the popularity of PPOs stems from the fact that patients have more choice between doctors whereas many people view HMO patients as being locked-in and having limited scope for changing doctors in the event of unsatisfactory service. The attraction of PPOs has led to a growth in their numbers of nearly 5 fold since 1983, so that by 1987 there were over 600 with an estimated 31 million enrolees. This means that PPOs now cater for rather more enrolees than all forms of HMO taken together.

Expenditure Control

Prior to the 1960s, the main concern of policy makers was to improve access to health care for those with inadequate insurance cover through the development of more comprehensive insurance programmes. These efforts culminated in major legislation being passed in 1965 to provide publicly financed benefits to elderly and low-income families through the Medicare and Medicaid programmes. However, while more comprehensive insurance increased access to health care, the growth of third party payments gave rise to another problem, cost inflation. Between 1960 and 1980 the proportion of GDP devoted to health expenditure increased from 5.2 to 9.2 per cent. During the 1980s the rate of growth has been more modest, but the trend has still been upwards. In 1987 total health spending accounted for 11.2 per cent of GDP. Efforts to contain rising expenditures on health care fall into two main categories: regulation and competition.

Regulation

During the late 1960s and early 1970s regulatory policy operated by state and/or federal government sought to control capital investment, utilisation, prices and the spread of new technology. Certificate of need (CON) legislation, for example, which was mandated on a federal basis in 1974, aimed to control the expansion of hospital and nursing home capacity. However, avoidance of controls was widespread and CON did little to restrict hospital investment; at best it succeeded in diverting it to more capital intensity per bed (Luft, 1985).

Peer review organisations (PROs) represent another form of regulatory mechanism. The forerunner of PROs — Professional Standards Review Organisations (PSROs) — were first established in 1972 with the aim of reviewing hospital utilisation for quality and appropriateness of treatment. These were replaced by a smaller number of PROs in 1981. Currently, they are used to monitor hospital services financed by Medicare and Medicaid in order to identify unnecessary treatment and to ensure quality of care. Evidence about their effectiveness is ambiguous. Some studies suggest that this monitoring has been responsible for substantial savings, while others reach different conclusions.

Of longer standing is the Joint Commission on the Accreditation of Health Care Organisations. The Joint Commission is an independent accreditation agency whose role is to promote high standards in hospitals and other health care facilities. Much of its work has focussed on the quality of the environment in which care is provided, but recently greater emphasis has been placed on clinical standards. As part of this, the Joint Commission is seeking to develop measures of clinical performance for use during hospital visits. At the same time, higher priority is being attached to the existence of effective arrangements for peer review within hospitals.

Competition

In the face of ambiguous evidence and — possibly more importantly — the changed political climate represented by the Reagan administration, policies for cost containment during the 1980s have relied on a different mechanism. Emphasis has been placed on market forces in the belief that greater competition will result in cost minimising behaviour. According to this view, a competitive environment within the health economy constitutes a more effective source of financial discipline than bureaucratic regulation.

A number of strategies have been followed with a view to increasing competition. Supply side policy has encouraged the development of HMOs in the belief that, through competition, they will force fee-for-service doctors to become more price sensitive. In addition, the Federal Trade Commission, by removing restraints on trade, such as bans on advertising, has played a major part in creating a more competitive environment. As a result, competition between insurance plans for subscribers and between hospitals for patient contracts is now quite intense.

On the demand side, the increased use of cost sharing has been designed to make consumers more aware of the cost of health services and to deter overuse. The hope is that discriminating consumers will be more resistant to price increases than government agencies or insurance companies.

While considerable attention has been focussed on the growth of competition during the 1980s, an equally, if not more, significant development has been the introduction of a new form of price regulation operated through the Medicare payments system. Prior to 1984, hospitals were paid for the services they provided in a retrospective, cost-based system. This gave hospitals an explicit incentive to increase spending, as more expenditure generated more revenue.

In 1984, however, Medicare introduced a prospective payments system (PPS) for its Part-A hospital programme. Now hospitals are paid a fixed price per case based on the diagnosis related group (DRG) case-mix system. Hospitals know what they are going to receive for treating a patient at the time of admission. Moreover their freedom to retain any surplus over the actual costs they incur, and, conversely, the risk of making a loss if they exceed the specified price, provides an incentive for keeping costs down.

Each year the government updates the level of payments to be made through PPS. This updating takes account of hospital price inflation and other factors such as changes in hospital productivity and the introduction of new technology. During the first two years of the system, the level of payments and their rate of increase were generally considered to offer most hospitals scope for generous profit margins. Subsequently, however, payments have been tightened as part of a conscious effort at cost containment. The government does not see its role as adjusting payments passively to increase costs, but as providing a payments structure which actively offers incentives for greater efficiency.

Has Expenditure Control been Successful?

During the early 1980s the advocates of competition were enthusiastic about its ability to control escalating cost inflation. Most of the subsequent evidence suggests that this optimism was misplaced. Health care spending has continued on its long-term upward trend. Part of the reason for this seems to be that, in the hospital sector, competition has not led to lower prices. Many hospitals have eschewed price competition and competed instead in terms of quality. This has actually served to increase prices in more competitive areas as hospitals have sought to offer a full range of expensive clinical facilities (Luft et al., 1986). Interestingly, though, some very recent evidence from California suggests that competition may have started to moderate the rate of hospital cost inflation (Melnick and Zwanziger, 1988). This shows that, in the post-1983 period, hospitals in competitive markets have experienced lower rates of cost increase than those in less competitive markets. However, it is probably too early to say whether this trend will be sustained.

As far as regulatory policies are concerned, Medicare PPS has almost certainly had a moderating influence on hospital costs of the elderly.

Hospital price inflation fell sharply between 1982 and 1985, and by 1986 was less than half the rate prevailing at the beginning of the 1980s. Similarly, numbers of inpatient admissions and average lengths of hospital stay have also fallen. But these moderating trends have been more than offset by cost increasing developments in other areas of health spending, including those resulting from strategies specifically designed to avoid PPS controls.

For example, because doctors' fees are not covered by PPS, but their freedom to undertake work in hospitals has been constrained through control of inpatient costs, there has been an increase in the number of outpatient and day surgery cases. Similarly much inpatient pre-admission diagnostic work has been shifted to doctors' offices outside hospital where it is not subject to PPS. Even within the PPS there is evidence of DRG 'creep': that is, the classification of patients into more costly DRG categories than is strictly necessary on clinical grounds, in order to increase hospital revenues. In addition, expenditure in areas not covered by PPS has been subject to increases in the intensity of treatment. In particular, the availability of expensive new medical technologies has meant that the quantity of inputs per case has tended to increase quite markedly, with a resultant rise in total spending.

The evidence also suggests that managed care has not been wholly successful as a cost containment strategy. Utilisation review programmes have certainly involved much closer examination of the appropriateness of treatment decisions and have reduced the freedom of doctors to practice autonomously. But doctors have often found ways around the controls that have been used, and this has frustrated attempts to limit overall levels of spending (Caper, 1988).

Faced with evidence of the limited impact of competition on total expenditure, some advocates of this strategy have claimed that it is inappropriate to expect it to limit costs (Pauly, 1989). A market, they argue, cannot be expected to minimise expenditure, but it can be expected to produce the right level of expenditure. This claim is based on the belief that markets provide an opportunity for consumers to reveal their preferences through individual spending decisions and provide an incentive structure for the supply of services to respond to these demands. According to this view, increased spending on health care is simply not a problem if that is what consumers want.

The Supply of Services and Consumer Choice

High levels of spending have resulted in high levels of service provision in many areas of health care, especially in the hospital sector. Aaron and

Shwartz (1984) show that, in comparison with the UK, the US:

• carries out twice as many X-ray examinations per person;

• offers more than three times the rate of kidney dialysis treatment;

• has six times the CT scanning capacity;

• performs ten times the rate of coronary artery surgery;

• has between five and ten times as many hospital intensive care beds.

Whether or not this level of service provision is a matter for congratulation or for concern is a hotly debated issue. Advocates of the market system claim that it is a result of myriad decisions freely undertaken by consumers. Nowadays Americans are offered an enormous range of insurance plans providing different levels of care and comprehensiveness. That many choose to pay levels of premiums entitling them to immediate treatment using the latest high technology equipment is, according to supporters of the system, a legitimate expression of consumer choice: a choice that is denied individuals in the UK where tight government expenditure constraints on the NHS lead to the rationing of care and waiting lists.

Critics, however, point to a tendency towards overspending because of supplier induced demand: that is, over utilisation resulting from the decisions of doctors who have a financial incentive to provide unnecessary services. As recent work on the appropriateness of medical care has shown, a significant proportion of treatment is either inappropriate or equivocal. This work uses panels of doctors to develop indicators of appropriate treatment for specified conditions and the indicators are then applied retrospectively to medical records. The evidence suggests that up to one third of medical and surgical procedures are performed inappropriately (Chassin et al., 1987). Additional evidence on the existence of supplier induced demand is offered by the work of Wennberg (1987) which shows that a major determinant of, for example, the rate of hospital admissions in an area, is the level of hospital services available and not the relative needs of the population.

Partly as a result of the profusion of health care technologies, there has been a major investment in technology assessment. The National Institute of Health makes a substantial investment in clinical trials and is also involved in organising consensus conferences. Within the federal government, the Food and Drugs Administration (FDA) regulates the introduction of new drugs and devices, and the approval of the FDA has to be obtained in advance of marketing. Also, the Office of Health Technology Assessment (OHTA) within the Department of Health and Human Services conducts evaluations of selected technologies to assist in decisions on whether particular technologies and procedures should be funded by Medicare.

OHTA is separate from the Office of Technology Assessment (OTA) which works to support Congress in identifying the beneficial and adverse impacts of the application of technology. OTA started on its health programmes in the mid 1970s and it undertakes both long and short term projects. OTA concentrates on data synthesis rather than original research and it works closely with external advisers and consultants in producing its reports.

Outside government, a number of the medical and specialist associations have undertaken technology assessments. Despite the wide range of activities of different agencies, there is a lack of coordination in the work that is done and no overall strategy linking the programmes of these agencies. Only recently, with the establishment of the Council on Health Care Technology under the aegis of the Institute of Medicine, has an attempt been made to overcome this. One of the main functions of the Council is to act as a clearing house for information on assessment activities.

Another contributory factor towards higher levels of hospital service provision — which is also largely a function of the way doctors choose to organise service delivery — is the proportionately small number of general practitioners. Americans frequently approach a specialist directly rather than, as in the UK, passing through a GP acting as a gatekeeper to more expensive specialist and hospital services. Indeed, one of the main advantages claimed by HMOs is an ability to manage care through the avoidance of costly and unnecessary hospital treatment, in much the same way as the British GP system does.

Ultimately, of course, judgements about the adequacy or otherwise of spending on health care should be based upon consideration of its impact on the health of the population. Unfortunately, this task is seriously hampered by the widespread lack of reliable evidence on the relationship between much medical treatment and health outcomes. Nonetheless, what evidence is available does not suggest that the health status of the US population is better as a result of the high levels of spending and service provision it offers.

International comparisons (OECD, 1987) show that, for example, the US has 12.8 infant deaths per thousand live births compared with 12.2 in the UK and an OECD average of 10.8. Similarly, life expectancy at birth in the US is 70.9 years compared with 71.3 in the UK and an OECD average of 71.7. Again, standardised death rates per hundred thousand population for infectious diseases and diseases of the circulatory system tend to be higher than average in the US, although the combined standardised death rate for all causes tends to be just below the OECD average. While this evidence is by no means conclusive — not least because health status depends on a far wider range of socio-economic variables than health spending per se — it does give pause for thought about the effectiveness of US levels of spending on health care.

Access to Health Services

Not everyone in the US has access to high levels of service provision, as the paradox of deprivation among excess demonstrates. The main reason is that many millions of Americans have no or inadequate health insurance.

It has been pointed out already that improving access to health care for those groups with inadequate insurance was a major policy concern during the 1960s, and that this led to the introduction of the Medicare and Medicaid programmes. During the late 1970s and early 1980s attention shifted more towards efficiency considerations: how to contain costs and control the inexorable rise in national health spending. One side effect of this policy emphasis has been a reduction in equity, as competition and other cost containment strategies have worsened access to health care for many people.

A number of the policies described already have contributed towards this state of affairs. Changes in Medicare have done so by controlling payments more tightly. In many states, payments on behalf of the poor — through the Medicaid programme — have been subjected to far more restrictive eligibility rules: fewer than 40 per cent of poor Americans are currently covered compared with 65 per cent 10 years ago. Private health insurance plans — in their efforts to attract enrolees through lower premiums — have become far more discriminating about the fees they will pay for hospital services. And, on the supply side, competition between hospitals has been encouraged as a means of meeting these demands for reduced costs.

The combined effect of all these measures has been to place increasing pressure on hospital finances. In some cases they are actually leading to bankruptcy and hospital closures. Since the early 1980s the number of hospitals closing each year has increased by about 50 per cent. Many of these closures are taking place in rural areas, often resulting in the communities affected having no access to nearby facilities. More generally, reduced profit margins (or surpluses over costs in the case of not-for-profit hospitals) have meant that private hospitals have been less able to engage in their traditional cross-subsidisation of patients who cannot meet their bills. This has made them less willing to treat the uninsured, with a resultant reduced access to care on the part of these groups.

Probably the most striking manifestation of this trend has been an increase in patient dumping: the practice of private hospitals sending patients home or to public hospitals when it becomes clear that they cannot meet their bills. Although most states have anti-dumping legislation, a recent congressional hearing was told that an estimated 250,000 patients are transferred from the emergency rooms of private hospitals to public hospitals annually solely for economic reasons.

Less dramatically, there is some research evidence which suggests that the trend towards cost sharing may have reduced access to care. A study by the prestigious RAND Institute (Newhouse et al., 1981) found that use of health care facilities tends to decline as the degree of cost sharing increases. They found that adults who had to share the cost of care made one third fewer ambulatory visits and were hospitalised about one third less often than individuals who received free care. These findings suggest that charging for health care constitutes a barrier to access to it, although a later RAND study indicated that individuals who received free care did not seem to be healthier because of it (Brook et al., 1983).

In response to these concerns about reduced access to health services on the part of large sections of the population, there have been a number of recent initiatives and proposals designed to extend insurance coverage. In the state of Massachussets, for example, a law was enacted in 1988 designed 'to make health security available to all citizens of the Commonwealth and to improve hospital financing'. The Act has two main features. First it created a department of medical security which will contract with private health insurance plans to make affordable coverage available to small businesses, most of whom presently do not offer health insurance to their employees. Second, the Act will impose a payroll tax on all firms with six or more workers. The revenues from this tax will be used to subsidise insurance for individuals not covered by employers' schemes.

Employer based insurance also plays a key role in a proposal for national health insurance recently put forward by Alain Enthoven (Enthoven and Kronick, 1989). In the Enthoven plan, all employers would be required to offer their employees insurance coverage and would be required to meet 80 per cent of the cost. They would also be required to pay a payroll tax. The proceeds of this tax would be used by public sponsors to meet 80 per cent of the cost of insurance of families not covered through employment. Families on low incomes would receive additional assistance in meeting the 20 per cent of insurance costs not covered by the sponsors' contribution, with those below the poverty line having their costs met in full.

Conclusion and Summary

In the review process leading up to the publication of Working for Patients, there is no doubt that ideas drawn from the United States played a powerful part in influencing Ministers' thinking. The work of Alain Enthoven, particularly his proposal for an internal market within the NHS (Enthoven, 1985), provided a model for NHS reform which was clearly consistent with the government's more general predisposition towards competitive market solutions. In view of the influence exerted by ideas emanating from US experience, it is important to establish the strengths and weaknesses of that system. In summary, the main strengths of the US system are:

- a considerable degree of patient choice between alternative insurance plans, health care schemes, doctors and hospitals;

- the widespread availability of the most up-to-date medical technology;

- a plentiful supply of hospital beds and medical staff, and an associated general absence of long waiting times for hospital admission;

- a flexible system with great diversity and a willingness to experiment and innovate.

Against these strengths, the main weaknesses are:

- spiralling health expenditures that are accounting for an ever growing share of GDP;

- an overemphasis on high-technology medical care at the expense of less costly, and possibly more efficacious, primary and community health services;

- extreme inequalities in access to health care with the uninsured dependent on often lower quality, public hospitals.

Thus, the United States exhibits many of the advantages and disadvantages associated with a market-based system. On the positive side, it includes financial incentives for the promotion of efficiency, offers a wide range of services offering considerable consumer choice, and a flexible system open to individualism and experimentation.

Against these advantages, however, it poses a number of problems. First, successive administrations have struggled with the inexorable rise in health care expenditures. At the present time, containing expenditure through tighter regulation of Medicare payments made on behalf of elderly people is an important policy priority. Other people, however, continue to place more reliance on the cost-containing merits of competitive markets in this connection, and point to recent Californian experience.

Second, there has been a continuing concern with quality of care and appropriateness of treatment. Both managed health care organisations and regulatory bodies, such as the Joint Commission on the Accreditation of Health Care Organisations, are continuing to develop strategies to improve quality and eliminate unnecessary treatments.

Finally, the US displays gross inequality of access to health care services. Numerous proposals for attacking this problem have been devised — usually involving the development of more comprehensive insurance arrangements — but, to date, few of them have attracted the necessary political support, no doubt because they all involve additional expenditure at a time when cost containment is seen as the primary policy goal.

6 Canada

Health services in Canada are mainly publicly financed and privately provided. The whole population is included in the public health scheme, funded through taxation, and encompassing all hospital and medical services. These services are delivered by private not-for-profit hospitals, and doctors who are private practitioners. Private finance is concentrated in those areas not included in the public scheme such as dental care and drugs required out of hospital.

With federal and provincial governments having assumed responsibility for health services finance, Canada offers a striking contrast to the United States. The contrast is even greater when it is realised that expenditure in Canada is considerably lower than in the United States and access to health care of different groups in the population is excellent. Problems have emerged in negotiations over doctors' fees and in waiting lists for some treatments, and there is also concern about the overemphasis placed on institutional care. But for the most part, services are of a high standard and public satisfaction with service provision compares favourably with that of other countries.

This chapter explores these issues by describing how health services are financed and provided, and it discusses the instruments used to control expenditure. The difficulty of controlling doctors' incomes is highlighted, and the extent to which patients are able to choose between providers is examined. The predominance of institutional care is emphasised, as is the use of acute hospital beds to provide care for elderly people. Attention then shifts to the management of clinical activity and to technology assessment. The penultimate section of the chapter focuses on health in Canada and assesses the impact of the Lalonde Report. Finally, the key strengths and weaknesses of health services in Canada are summarised.

The Financing and Provision of Services

Canada provides comprehensive health services to all of its population through a mixture of public and private finance. Health services expenditure comprised 8.6 per cent of GDP in 1987. 76 per cent of expenditure derived from public sources and all hospital and medical services are included in the public scheme.

Responsibility for financing health services in the public sector is shared between federal government and the ten provincial governments. Although Canada is sometimes said to have a national health insurance system, Barer et al. have noted:

> the distinctively Canadian form of financing is more accurately described as a federal-provincial system of public reimbursement for the costs of hospital and medical care, most of which is provided by private medical practitioners and not-for-profit hospitals. The former are paid fees for their services, the latter receive annual negotiated global budgets. The public reimbursement plans are run by each of the ten Canadian provinces, and cover the entire population for the costs of all medically necessary care, ambulatory or institutional (1988, p. 7).

As this comment indicates, it is at the provincial level that the main responsibility for health services lies. While there are sufficient common features between the provinces to enable an analysis of health services in Canada as a whole to be undertaken, it should be recognised that the details of health services delivery vary from province to province, making generalisations difficult.

Government finance for health care is derived principally from general taxation levied at the federal and provincial levels. Approximately 40 per cent of expenditures are met by federal government, although the exact proportion varies between provinces. Two provinces retain a system of health insurance premiums but these are de facto a form of general taxation. Private expenditure is concentrated in particular sectors of health care, the most significant of which are dentistry, drugs required out of hospital, and nursing homes. The provincial governments provide some funding for these services, especially for pensioners and those in receipt of social security. Part of the costs are also met from employer-sponsored insurance. But most private expenditure takes the form of direct payments by patients. It should be noted that private insurers are not allowed to offer insurance for services included the public scheme. This is an important difference from the UK and helps to explain the limited market for private insurance.

There are no user charges in the case of health services funded by the public sector. For a number of years, doctors in some provinces were able to charge patients a fee in addition to the payment they received from the government. But 'extra billing' as it is known has disappeared as a result of legislation passed in 1984 (see below).

Most hospitals in Canada are run on a not-for-profit basis. Each hospital has a board of trustees, and in some provinces the members of the board include appointees of the provincial government. Hospitals are funded through prospective budgets provided almost entirely by government, and capital expenditures have to be approved by government. Although the ownership of most hospitals is in private hands, in practice they are under a good deal of public influence.

The vast majority of doctors, both GPs and specialists, are private practitioners. As with hospitals, these doctors derive their incomes from government. The most common form of payment is fee-for-service and the fee schedule in set in periodic negotiations between provincial governments and medical associations.

Expenditure Control

Expenditure on health services in Canada has stabilised at around 8.5 per cent of GDP in the mid-1980s. As in Holland and West Germany, the government is unable to control total expenditure completely, but it is able to influence some of the main components of spending. The most important instruments available to government are prospective budgets for hospitals, controls over capital investment, and negotiations over doctors' fees. In tandem with the elimination of extra billing by doctors, these instruments have largely succeeded in bringing costs under control. As Evans (1986) has commented:

> the Canadian record of long-run cost stability ... has been the result of direct controls, such as face-to-face bargaining between physicians' representatives and the payers for care, and global budgeting for hospitals. Total spending is not completely locked in, as the volume of servicing by physicians is an uncontrolled variable, and hospitals can occasionally work their way around the 'globe'. But the scope for manipulating billing patterns is surprisingly limited when the structure of the fee schedule is itself negotiated (p. 603).

In this respect, Canada offers a striking contrast with its neighbour the United States (see figure 3). As Evans (1986) has demonstrated, health services expenditure in Canada and the United States grew in parallel until the introduction of universal, comprehensive, public financing of health care in Canada. This method of funding enabled Canada to provide health services to its entire population while at the same time limiting expenditure.

Figure 3   Health Expenditure as Share of GNP, Canada and USA, 1948–85

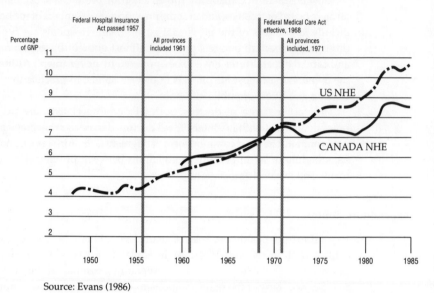

Source: Evans (1986)

In contrast, expenditure in the United States increased rapidly in the 1970s and 1980s amounting to 11.2 per cent of GDP in 1987. The rate of increase was particularly fast in the case of hospital services. An analysis of the use of hospitals in the United States and Canada indicates that higher levels of expenditure in the United States cannot be explained by differences in admission rates and case mix. Far more important is the greater intensity of treatment in the United States (Newhouse et al., 1988). In addition, payments to doctors are much higher in the United States, and a bigger proportion of the budget is allocated to administration and transaction costs (Evans, 1988).

Doctors' Incomes

Despite Canada's success in achieving overall expenditure control, the increase in doctors' incomes has been a continuing cause of concern to government. Doctors' fees are negotiated periodically by the provincial governments and medical associations. These negotiations serve to limit the fees paid for particular services but they are open-ended in that they place no limits on the number of services for which doctors are able to claim reimbursement. Expenditure is therefore determined by how doctors respond to the fees that are agreed, and in particular whether they increase utilisation rates. The available evidence suggests that utilisation rates have risen rapidly (more so in Canada than in the US), and that doctors have responded to limits on fees by doing more work (Barer et al., 1988).

Provincial governments have responded in turn by seeking firmer controls over total expenditure on doctors' services. As Lomas et al. (1989) have noted, two broad approaches have been pursued. First, there is the threshold approach which limits expenditure by reducing fees when utilisation rates exceed a pre-determined level. This approach has been used in British Columbia, Manitoba, Saskatchewan and Ontario. Second, there is the capping approach which controls expenditure by specifying personal incomes' ceilings for doctors and overall spending limits on doctors' fees. This approach has been used in Quebec. As these developments indicate, there are clear parallels between Canada, Holland and West Germany in the way doctors' fees are handled.

Evidence on the impact of these controls is inconclusive. The nature of doctors' contracts is in a considerable state of flux and the long-term outcome is unclear. What is certain is that provincial governments are taking a close interest in total expenditure on doctors' fees and now see this as at least as important as the detailed structure of the fee schedule. Also, in British Columbia, the provincial government has sought to limit the rate at which doctors set up in practice in an attempt to contain spending (Barer et al., 1988). Although this move failed, it indicates the way in which policy makers are responding to concern about doctors' fees.

Current negotiations are shaped by debates in the early 1980s about user charges levied by doctors. The medical associations have argued that these charges provide a safety valve to enable doctors to recoup income 'lost' in negotiations over fees. Against this, advocates of the public finance of services feared that charges might be exploited by conservative governments to reduce their expenditure on health services and to undermine the principle of equal access to health care.

The result was a bitter political debate culminating in the passage of the Canada Health Act in 1984. Under this Act, federal government's contribution to provincial governments was reduced dollar for dollar by each dollar of direct charges to patients either imposed or permitted by the provincial governments. As a consequence, user charges were eliminated, although not without strong opposition on the part of doctors, including a strike in Ontario (Stevenson et al., 1988). Underlying medical opposition to government policy was the claim that the autonomy of doctors would be eroded if they were denied the right to charge patients for their services.

Consumer Choice and Provider Competition

Patients have a wide choice of doctors and hospitals. Waiting lists for treatment are shorter than in the UK, although they have become more of a concern in recent years. Hospitals compete with each other for a share of government funding for services but this is part of the political process rather than a response to the incentives of the market place. In this process, hospitals have been relatively successful in obtaining resources, and the provincial governments have not used their purchasing power to press for improvements in performance.

Budgets for hospitals are not related directly to workload and so there is no financial incentive to attract additional patients. Indeed, hospitals have an incentive to limit the amount and intensity of work done in order to keep within budget. This can create conflict between hospital managers and doctors as the latter do have an incentive to increase their workload in response to fee-for-service reimbursement. International evidence suggests that rates of service provision are relatively high in Canada, illustrating again the phenomenon of supplier induced demand (Rachlis and Kushner, 1989).

One of the consequences of the different incentives faced by doctors and hospitals is that hospital expenditure may exceed budget and in the past governments have usually financed the deficit. However, this is no longer always the case, and hospitals have been forced to examine more closely their use of resources. This represents an important change in the incentive structure facing hospitals. Instead of expanding activity and running a deficit, knowing that this will be picked up by government, hospitals are increasingly questioning clinical practices and striving for higher levels of efficiency. A considerable investment is going into the development of information systems, and there is growing interest in the closer involvement of doctors and nurses in hospital management (see below).

In the case of doctors, ever increasing physician supply could in the future lead to greater competition for patients. To date, however, doctors' workloads have not fallen even though the patient-to-doctor ratio has declined. This is in part due to a rising proportion of the population visiting doctors, but more importantly patients are increasingly seeing more than one doctor for each treatment episode. In other words, the profession's response to an increased supply of providers has been to co-operate to share patients and to maintain incomes. However, this is likely to change as restrictions on doctors' fees create an incentive for doctors to do more work themselves and to limit referrals to colleagues.

In the light of United States experience, there is little enthusiasm in

Canada for competition based on private sector finance. On the other hand, there has been some interest in Ontario in the development of public sector competition, adapting HMO methods of organising services to a system of universal public coverage. This builds on existing Health Service Organisations (HSOs) which involve groups of doctors paid on a capitation basis to provide services to their patients. The reimbursement of these doctors includes an incentive to provide care within the HSO rather than referring on to a specialist.

There has been some debate about whether HSOs could compete effectively with traditional fee-for-service practice, although there is no experience as yet of efforts to stimulate such competition. In a health service in which patients are not charged at the point of use and have a free choice of practitioner, there are no obvious ways of building in an incentive for patients to choose HSOs. Indeed, in 1986 only 2 per cent of the population in Ontario were enrolled with HSOs.

The Balance of Care

One of the reasons behind the interest in new forms of delivery is the perceived need to shift the balance of care away from hospitals. Historically, Canada has spent a high percentage of its budget on institutional care, especially hospitals. OECD analysis of the financing and delivery of health care shows that institutional spending comprised 59 per cent of public health spending in the 1980s, compared with an OECD mean of 54 per cent. Nevertheless, this represents a marked reduction in the proportion of the budget allocated to institutional care since 1970 when the comparable figures were 67 per cent in Canada in relation to an OECD mean of 51 per cent. The controls exercised over hospital spending since the introduction of public financing of health services and global budgets help to explain this reduction.

OECD data also demonstrate that average lengths of stay have increased in the same period. Canada is the only country in which this has occurred. These data should, however, be interpreted with caution. In a number of countries, long term care facilities are included in the analysis, and this makes comparison between systems difficult.

Long term care is not part of the public health service in Canada and arrangements vary between provinces. The uneven provision of nursing homes and related facilities means that acute hospital beds are used for long term care in some places. As a number of commentators have noted (Iglehart, 1986; Evans, 1986), the effect is that hospital beds are inappropriately occupied, and there is concern that resources are not always used optimally.

The use of acute hospitals for long term care is one of the factors which helps to explain the differences in hospital spending between Canada and the US noted above. That is, Canada's lower levels of hospital expenditure can be attributed in part to the use of acute beds for the treatment of elderly people whose daily care requirements are below average (Evans et al., 1989). Although this serves to limit expenditure, it does not necessarily represent an effective use of resources. In recognition of this, developments are underway in a number of provinces to build up services outside hospitals in order to reduce the use of hospitals for long term care. These developments include providing home care and community care as well as increasing nursing home provision.

This has not emerged as a particularly significant problem to date because the proportion of the population aged over 65 is relatively low in Canada at 9.5 per cent compared with an OECD mean of 12.2 per cent in 1980. However, population projections indicate a significant change in the next century. By 2030, over 22 per cent of the population is expected to be over the age of 65, and this is likely to have major financial and service implications.

In response to demographic projections and to concern about the predominance of hospital care, provincial governments have sought to encourage the development of alternative services, such as the Health Service Organisations discussed above. In addition, Community Health Centres have been established in Ontario to provide primary care to special needs groups, and these centres are funded through global budgets. Similarly, Local Centres for Community Services have been set up in Quebec to deliver primary care and social services, and in the same province there have been experiments with hospital- at-home schemes.

More radically, a report on health services in Ontario published in 1987 put forward a range of ideas on future developments including extramural hospitals, hospital organised home care, and an extended role for HSOs to encompass a full range of specialist care as well as primary care (Evans, 1987). Behind these proposals was the view that new forms of organisation and incentives were required to encourage the provision of services appropriate to the needs of patients. In addition, it was argued that better value for money would be obtained if less emphasis were placed on hospital services and higher priority were given to primary and community care. Lack of integration between different sectors was perceived to be a key challenge for policy makers as health care and social services entered the 1990s.

In one respect, health services already contain an incentive to limit expenditure on hospital and specialist services. This is contained within the fee schedule for doctors under which specialists receive the higher fee for specialist consultations only if there is a referral from a GP and a report back to the referring physician. GPs thus act as gatekeepers, although they have an incentive to refer frequently in that they then have more time to spend on other patients, thereby earning additional fees. Against this, as pressure on doctors' fees increases, and provincial governments seek to cap expenditure, the provision of extra services by specialists is likely to reduce the amount of money available to GPs. As this happens, GPs will be more likely to limit referrals and to take direct responsibility for patient care, especially if proposals to develop primary care services funded through capitation payments gain ground.

Managing Clinical Activity

As we noted above, Canadian hospitals are usually run by a board of trustees. Day-to-day management is in the hands of a chief executive, and there is usually a chief of medical staff employed on a salaried basis. In larger hospitals, there will also be chiefs of major clinical services, or clinical directors. Doctors who have admitting privileges are private practitioners and they are organised as the hospital's medical staff. In practice, management responsibility is usually shared between the board of trustees, the chief executive and the medical staff.

Doctors in Canada enjoy considerable freedom to practise in the way they consider appropriate. Subject only to the overall constraints imposed by global hospital budgets and the fee schedule, each doctor is able to determine the place and form of treatment for his patients. In this respect, Canadian doctors are in a similar position to their UK counterparts, although the existence of chiefs of medical staff and of clinical services has created a clearer structure for the organisation of medical work. This structure involves an element of hierarchy between doctors in which the ultimate sanction is the withdrawal of admitting privileges for doctors whose practices are deemed to be unacceptable. The Canadian approach to medical management enables chiefs of staff to encourage their colleagues to participate in peer review and themselves to assess performance by analysing data gathered for reimbursement purposes.

There is growing interest in the involvement of doctors in management (LeTouze, 1986) and in achieving closer integration between hospital management and clinical activity. As we noted earlier, this is partly a response to increasing financial constraints and to the different set of incentives faced by managers and doctors. Although there has been little experience of clinical budgeting, some of the new structures which are emerging — for example, at Sunnybrook Hospital in Toronto — closely parallel those which exist at Guy's Hospital and other large teaching hospitals in the US and Europe (Weaver, 1988; Sunnybrook Report, 1988).

These structures are making use of increasingly sophisticated clinical information systems, including DRGs, to compare performance in different hospitals. However there is no inclination at all to move towards DRG reimbursement for hospitals. The main reason for this is that workload funding based on DRGs is perceived to be likely to increase expenditure compared with global budgets.

In the case of hospitals, there is a national accreditation agency, the Canadian Council of Health Facilities Accreditation (CCHFA), which operates on a voluntary basis. The Council is a non-governmental agency and its board members are drawn from the Canadian Medical Association, the Canadian Hospital Association, the Canadian Nurses Association, the Royal College of Physicians and Surgeons, and the Canadian Long Term Care Association. Hospitals apply to the CCHFA for accreditation and pay a fee to cover the costs of a visit and report by a survey team. Team members are nurses, doctors and administrators on secondment from the health service. During their inspections, teams make use of standards developed with assistance from member organisations.

Standards and guidelines have also been developed by the Department of National Health and Welfare. The guidelines' programme has been in operation since 1972 and it involves the use of expert working groups to produce a comprehensive outline of requirements for services in health institutions. To date, guidelines have been published on a wide range of services including day surgery, magnetic resonance imaging and stroke services.

In comparison with the United States, new and expensive health care technologies disseminate less rapidly in Canada. However, as Evans has noted:

> the system of global constraint through political process creates no inherent demand, by providers or payers, for sound evaluation of the effectiveness of current practices. Neither side in the dialogue has thus far shown any great interest in taking the risks implicit in a serious scientific evaluation of either current practices or new proposals (1986, p. 603).

While Evans' observation continues to hold true, there has been growing interest in the development of technology assessment in recent years. For example, a consensus conference on the use of caesarian sections was held in 1986, a Council of Health Technology Assessment has been established in Quebec, and an Institute for Health Care Facilities of the Future has been set up to examine, among other things, the impact of developments in health care technology on health services.

Despite these efforts, there have been renewed calls for a more co-ordinated approach, including a proposal to establish a National Health Technology Assessment Council (Stoddart and Feeny, 1986). As critics have argued, much medical treatment is unproven in its effectiveness; there is evidence to suggest excessive levels of servicing compared with other countries; and there may be scope for substantial savings through the adoption of more cost-effective forms of care. One estimate puts these savings as high as $12 billion (£6.3 billion) out of a total budget of $46 billion (£24 billion) (Rachlis and Kushner, 1989). As pressure on government to allocate extra resources to health care mounts, it is likely that the efficiency with which existing budgets are used will receive greater attention.

Health in Canada

Canadians enjoy good health in terms of available indicators. Infant mortality rates and life expectancy are better than the OECD average. Moreover, there has been considerable interest in the promotion of good health. This is exemplified by the Lalonde Report, *A New Perspective on the Health of Canadians*, published in 1974 by the federal government (Lalonde, 1974). The report, which gained worldwide recognition, called for a re-orientation of health services away from curative medicine to the prevention of illness and disease. Although the thinking behind the Lalonde Report has had some impact, much remains to be done to achieve the shift in resources argued for by Lalonde.

At federal level, public health policy has been taken forward through the Health Promotion Directorate. With a staff of over 100, the Directorate has provided a focus for action across in Canada. To a large extent, the work of the Directorate has sought to influence lifestyle and behaviour as a means of improving health. More recently, federal government committed itself to achieving Health for All (Epp, 1986), and this approach has found echoes in some of the provinces (for example, Spasoff, 1987).

At the local level, arrangements for public health vary from province to province. In Quebec, departments of community health are based in acute hospitals (Pollock, 1989). Elsewhere, public health is usually the responsibility of provincial and local government. This is the arrangement in the city of Toronto in Ontario. Toronto is part of WHO's Healthy Cities network and the city government has a mandate to make Toronto the healthiest city in North America by the year 2000 (Ashton and Seymour, 1988).

Despite the progress made at the provincial and local levels, health promotion continues to receive relatively low priority overall (LeTouze, 1986). Furthermore, it is often behavioural and lifestyle factors that are emphasised by government, rather than collective action. This is well illustrated by the Ontario Health Review (Evans, 1987) which identified a stronger role for the *individual* in improving health as one of three key issues for the future. Similarly, although federal policy has shifted away from an emphasis on lifestyle and behaviour to embrace social, economic and environmental influences on health (Raeburn, 1987), the most recent restatement of policy identifies self care and mutual aid as two of the key mechanisms intrinsic to health promotion (Epp, 1986).

In short, despite the impact of the Lalonde Report outside Canada, it has had an uneven influence within the country. As Evans (1982) has argued, this can be attributed to the wide range of interpretations that can be placed on the report. From federal government's point of view, the 'New Perspective' justified limitations on health spending and an emphasis on personal responsibility for health. New government initiatives have been taken but their significance is more symbolic than real. The Lalonde Report was much more effective in identifying problems than in suggesting solutions, and the bulk of expenditure continues to be devoted to mainstream medical care programmes.

Conclusion and Summary

Analysis of health services in Canada indicates that it is possible to provide comprehensive services to the whole population through tax funding with choice for patients. At around 8.5 per cent of GDP, expenditure on health services is similar to that in Holland and West Germany, and lower than in Sweden and the United States. For this expenditure, patients have access to a wide range of providers on the basis of need, and all groups in the population are covered. Furthermore, the evidence suggests that Canadians are well satisfied with their health services and view their system more positively than consumers in either the United States or the United Kingdom. This emerged clearly from a survey conducted in 1988 which demonstrated that Canadians have a high opinion of their health service and are less likely than their counterparts in the UK and the US to feel that fundamental changes are needed (Blendon, 1989).

In summary, the strengths of health services in Canada are:

- the provision of comprehensive services to the whole population on the basis of need;

- access to care is good and there is limited waiting for treatment;

- there is a large measure of control over total expenditure;

- patients have a wide choice between doctors and hospitals;

- doctors are becoming increasingly involved in management and there is considerable experience of medical audit and accreditation.

The main weaknesses of the system are:

- a strong emphasis on hospital care;

- an underdeveloped system of care outside hospitals, for example in nursing homes, in the community and in people's own homes;

- a lack of incentives for efficiency on the part of hospitals and doctors;

- the failure of provincial governments as purchasers of care to use their power over providers to press for greater efficiency in service delivery;

- the difficulty in controlling doctors' incomes when incomes are based on fee-for-service, and the incentive this method of payment creates for over servicing;

- a limited investment in technology assessment.

In conclusion, health services in Canada emerge relatively well from comparative analysis. As Iglehart (1986) noted in his assessment:

> the health care systems of Western industrialised nations are shaped largely by a commitment to several essential but competing values: ready access, high quality and reasonable cost. Canada has developed a provincially administered health insurance scheme that generally achieves all three of these goals (p. 778).

Evans has argued that the key to Canada's success is the control over finance exercised by government. It is this which enables government to limit expenditure on hospital and medical services and to ensure comprehensive coverage. The corollary is that greater pluralism in funding and provision would result in an escalation in expenditure, as has occurred in the United States (Evans, 1984). As Evans argues:

> one can have restraint as in Canada, in a payment system which has various free-choice dimensions, so long as one maintains sole-source funding. If it were possible for private insurance companies acting in conjunction with physicians and private hospitals to 'cream-off' low risk groups in Canada, it is highly unlikely that expenditure could have been contained during the 1970s. The public monopoly on the insurance and reimbursement is the critical control lever (p. 406).

There is nevertheless a price to be paid for the achievements of the Canadian system. In particular, pressures are emerging between federal and provincial governments over responsibility for funding, and between provincial governments and medical associations over doctors' incomes. This has given rise in turn to debate about future options, including the provision of additional funding by government, the reintroduction of user charges, a reversion to private insurance, and the introduction of managed competition drawing on United States experience of HMOs (Evans, 1984). However, given the popularity of health services with the public, and the salutary example of the United States, a major change of direction appears unlikely. Much more probable are incremental adjustments within existing arrangements for financing and provision in order to tackle the weaknesses that are widely acknowledged to exist.

7

Conclusions

The Prime Minister's Review of the NHS, and the resulting white paper, have stimulated a fundamental reappraisal of health services finance and delivery. In this chapter, we draw together the main findings of our analysis, and examine the relevance of international experience for the continuing debate about the future of health services in the UK. In particular, we assess the evidence on alternative methods of funding, and discuss different approaches to the delivery of services. This includes reviewing the impact of competition among providers and the effectiveness of government planning and regulation. Finally, we examine public health policy, identifying the implications for the UK of the strategies pursued in other countries.

Health Services Finance

Although the financing of health services was actively discussed in the first part of the Prime Minister's Review, no major change was proposed in the white paper. Having reviewed the options, the government decided to retain the existing method of funding through taxation and came down against a move towards social insurance or private insurance. The one exception was the offer of tax relief on health insurance premiums for the over 60s. However, private insurance will remain a minor supplement to tax funding.

Because the white paper did not address the issue of funding, it seems certain that health services finance will emerge again before too long as an issue of debate. Despite some signs of a more favourable funding position in the immediate future, the underlying problem of a political system seemingly unable to deliver the volume of health care services people appear to want will persist. What, then, are the main alternatives to funding based on taxation? And would these alternatives help to tackle the difficulties that have arisen in the UK?

All of the countries we have studied rely on a mixture of sources to fund health services. Nevertheless, three broad approaches to funding can be identified. The first, represented by the United States, draws mainly on private finance supported by a public safety net for those on low incomes and elderly people. The second, represented by Canada, Sweden and also the UK, uses public funds raised through taxation to provide services for the whole population. The third, represented by West Germany and Holland, is characterised by a mixture of compulsory social insurance and private insurance. The Dutch approach is more pluralistic than the German, particularly in excluding higher income groups from all but the basic social insurance for catastrophic illness.

The evidence suggests that systems which rely heavily on private finance have considerable difficulty in controlling overall expenditure. This is certainly the case in the United States where the upward trend in the proportion of GDP allocated to health services is a continuing cause of concern. United States experience also demonstrates the difficulty of achieving equitable access to services when private insurance is the main source of funding. The gaps in cover that exist in the United States and the wide variations in access to services experienced by different individuals suggest that this is not a method of funding that should be copied in the UK.

Canadian and Swedish experience offers a striking contrast to the United States. In both countries, expenditure has been brought under control, and the whole population has access to a comprehensive range of services. The Canadian evidence indicates that the introduction of universal, comprehensive public financing of health care was of decisive importance in achieving long run cost stability. Although expenditure as a proportion of GDP has increased in Canada in the 1980s, cost control has been far more effective than in the United States. Similarly, in Sweden, agreements between national government and the county councils to limit increases in spending led to a fall in the proportion of the GDP allocated to health services in the mid- 1980s, albeit from a relatively high level. The importance of tax funding as a control mechanism is reinforced by experience in the UK where health services consumed a fairly constant 6 per cent of GDP during the 1980s.

However, the ability to control expenditure can itself give rise to problems if the result is a health service unable to provide sufficient services to meet the perceived needs of the population. This has been the situation in both Sweden and particularly the UK, and it lies behind demands for increased financing of health services in these countries. Public expenditure constraints also help to explain rising subscriptions to private health insurance in Sweden and the UK. Canada has so far largely escaped these pressures, although the effect of budgetary restrictions has emerged in the political process in disputes between federal and provincial governments over their respective responsibilities for funding, and in demands from the medical associations for increases in doctors' fees.

In theory, social insurance offers a middle way between tax financing and private insurance. In essence, social insurance is an earmarked tax levied on a narrower tax base than general taxation. Individuals are able to see that their contribution is spent on health services, contributions can be increased or controlled in response to public pressure, and in some countries (for example, West Germany) certain people can opt out of the state scheme if they prefer to make their own arrangements. It is also possible to build in a safety net to ensure that the costs of catastrophic illness will be met and that those out of work or on low incomes have coverage. In this way, the access of different groups in the population to services can be assured, and it is possible to avoid many of the problems of underinsurance that have arisen in the United States.

The evidence from Holland and West Germany shows that expenditure as a proportion of GDP has broadly stabilised in recent years. In Holland, this has been achieved mainly through prospective budgets for hospitals, limits on doctors' fees, controls over the number of new beds and building, and restrictions on the use of health care technology. In West Germany, government has sought to limit the increase in contributions to the social insurance funds by capping expenditure on doctors' fees, extending user charges, introducing prospective budgets for hospitals and restricting the services available through the social insurance scheme. A distinctive feature of the German approach is the degree to which responsibility for staying within budget limits rests with doctors acting collectively.

Despite the success of these countries in controlling the rate of growth in expenditure, there are a number of problems with social insurance funding. First, increases in insurance contributions have been a cause of concern, particularly when these have been used to finance a system of health care in which there is evidence of inefficiency and over provision. This applies particularly in West Germany where average contributions are almost 13 per cent of income divided between employees and employers. Payments at this level have added considerably to labour costs, as well as imposing a financial burden on employees. In both West Germany and Holland, there are moves to limit the resources available to the sick funds in order to stimulate the funds to use their resources more efficiently. Steps are also being taken to increase user charges to make consumers more aware of the expense of health care.

Second, Dutch experience shows that inequities can arise when social insurance and private insurance operate in tandem. In Holland, individuals who are just below the income level for entry into private insurance usually pay more for their insurance cover than individuals above the income level who are able to negotiate lower payments with private insurers. Furthermore, private insurers have become more careful in selecting risks, discriminating against elderly people and those in poor health. Partly in response to these difficulties, the Dutch government is introducing a unified compulsory social insurance scheme providing basic services to all for a fixed premium. This will be supplemented by voluntary insurance for services not included in the basic package. Insurers will be obliged to accept patients to avoid risk selection; and individuals will have some choice over the extent of their cover.

Third, German experience points to the inequities that can arise when social insurance is administered through sick funds which set different contribution rates and yet provide essentially the same range of services. People in West Germany contribute between 8 and 16 per cent of income to the sick funds, the exact proportion depending on the risks represented by the membership of the fund concerned. As a consequence, white collar workers tend to be in a more favourable position than blue collar workers and people on low incomes. A major concern in West Germany at present is to achieve equalisation between the funds in order to reduce the variations in contribution rates.

Figure 4   Total Health Expenditure as Share of GDP

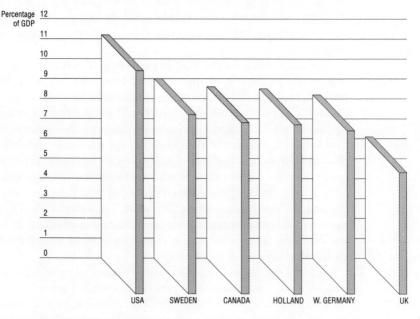

Source: Schieber and Poullier (1989)

A further consideration is that social insurance is a more regressive form of funding than general taxation. Individuals pay the same percentage contribution whatever their income, and this imposes a bigger burden on lower-income groups than tax funding.

The conclusion we draw from these comparisons is that all methods of financing have their weaknesses. Tax funding has many advantages, not least in enabling expenditure to be controlled, promoting equity and access, and allowing services to be provided to the whole population, but in the UK it has failed to deliver the volume of resources needed to finance services to the level demanded by the public (Jowell et al., 1988). Although there is no scientific way of determining what the right level of expenditure should be — this is, after all, a matter of political judgement — it is clear that the UK spends considerably less on health services than other countries. This is illustrated in Figure 4.

Much of the difference in spending between countries is accounted for by differences in national income (Maxwell, 1981 and 1988). Nevertheless, expenditure in the UK is still lower than would be expected by international comparisons. While some of the difference is the result of relatively low levels of private expenditure on health services, as displayed by

Figure 5   Public and Private Expenditure on Health as Share of Total, 1987

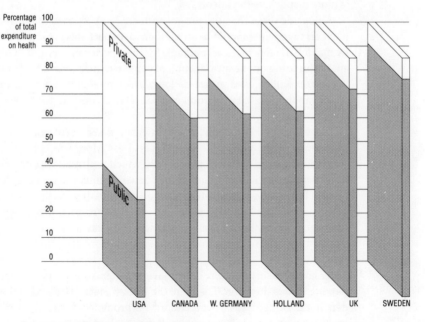

Source: Schieber and Poullier (1989)

Figure 5, there is also an under investment in terms of public expenditure (Robinson et al., 1988).

This suggests if tax funding is to be retained, expenditure should be increased to meet the shortfall that exists. On the other hand, if a switch to social insurance is seriously contemplated, then careful thought will have to be given to the design of the system to avoid the difficulties that have arisen elsewhere. If these difficulties can be overcome, social insurance may well offer an effective means of channelling additional resources into the health services.

Health Services Delivery

The government's plans for the future of the NHS will bring about major changes to the delivery of health services. In particular, the providers of services will have to compete for funds from health authorities, GP budget holders and private sources. To this end, responsibility for funding and provision will be separated, and hospitals and other services will be encouraged to opt out of health authority control to become self-governing NHS trusts. In effect, public funds will be used to purchase care on a contract basis from a range of providers in different sectors, and the government hopes that this will lead to greater efficiency and a service that is more responsive to patients.

Alongside these changes, the government has proposed that management arrangements should be strengthened. In part, this is to be achieved by making doctors more accountable for their performance, and in part it entails building on the introduction of general management. In this way, regulation will be used in association with competition in a programme which amounts to the most fundamental set of changes to the NHS since its inception.

In the light of this agenda for reform, what can be learnt from overseas experience of the delivery of health services? More specifically, what conclusions can be drawn from countries which have made use of competition between providers? And what policy instruments have been developed in those countries which have relied on regulation? Is the UK in step with international developments, or are the government's proposals unusual in the context of changes taking place elsewhere?

Competition

Three countries in our study either have experience of competition or are moving in this direction. These are the United States, Holland and Sweden. In the United States, competition was promoted during the 1980s as an instrument for containing costs. Policy makers under successive Reagan administrations argued that market forces would be more effective than bureaucratic regulation in slowing the rate of growth in spending. In fact, as we showed in chapter 5, evidence at the macro-level does not suggest that competition policy has succeeded in this respect. Indeed, policy makers have increasingly supplemented competitive mechanisms with regulatory instruments such as the prospective payments system (see below).

It is difficult to make predictions about the UK from United States experience because of major differences between the two systems in terms of methods and levels of funding and the ownership of hospitals. In particular, the dominance of private finance and private provision, the much higher level of expenditure, and the limited role of government mean that competition has developed under quite different conditions. Although there are clear warnings from the United States in the failure to guarantee access to health care for all and evidence of patient dumping by hospitals, it should not be assumed that these weaknesses are an inevitable by-product of competition. Provided that adequate safeguards are established, there is no reason in principle why competition should not be used to promote greater efficiency in health care delivery. And, in fact, this is precisely what is being attempted in Holland and Sweden.

The Dekker reforms in Holland seek to introduce a market-oriented approach into a social insurance system. Vulnerable groups will be protected by being included in the basic insurance arrangements, and insurers will be obliged to accept patients. Like HMOs in the United States, insurers will have a fixed budget and they will have an incentive to use their resources efficiently and to provide services that attract subscribers. One of the aims of these reforms is to strengthen the position of the purchasers of care vis-a-vis providers and to encourage selective contracting by purchasers. Another objective is to enable consumers to choose between competing insurers.

As yet there is no experience of competition in operation in Holland as the Dekker report is in the process of being implemented in stages. Nevertheless, in the debate on Dekker, there are clear echoes of discussion in the UK in the wake of the Prime Minister's Review. More specifically, concerns have been aired about the ability of purchasers to negotiate contracts with providers, the extent to which competition will occur when providers in some areas have a monopoly, and uncertainty about the impact of the reforms on the quality of care. Also, despite assurances about protecting the right to health care of groups such as the elderly and those on low incomes, doubts persist about the adequacy of the reforms in this area. The way in which policy makers respond to these concerns will be of considerable relevance to the UK, and we discuss below the need to strengthen the capacity for learning between different systems.

Changes taking place in the Swedish health service also include elements of competition. Like the NHS, the Swedish system is dominated by public finance and public provision, and only recently have market-oriented ideas gained currency. These ideas centre on the use of financial incentives to encourage hospitals and doctors in the public sector to be more responsive to consumers. Although experience of these arrangements is extremely limited, they are of interest because they have emerged in the one country in our study which has traditionally placed a high value on government planning and shown least interest in competition.

It is worth adding that competition may also become a more important factor in the West German health service in future. To date, there has been little competition, one of the reasons being that resources have been available to fund a generous level of service provision. A further factor is that sick funds have sought to attract members by offering a wide choice of providers and have been reluctant to put hospitals in the position of competing for their business. There is some prospect that this will change as expenditure controls are tightened and as the federal government seeks to encourage the sick funds to contract selectively with providers and use those hospitals that are most efficient.

Regulation

Three issues in health care regulation are particularly relevant for the UK. These concern the management of clinical activity, the balance between institutional care and community care, and the use of global budgets.

In all countries there is interest in the management of clinical activity as efforts are made to involve doctors, nurses and other health care professionals in management. At one level, this interest is reflected in work on resource management, with developments in Sweden, Canada and Holland paralleling activity in the UK. These developments vary from country to country, but they include a concern to give hospital doctors more responsibility for management, to establish clinical budgets, and to develop information systems capable of providing doctors and managers with improved data about the cost and outcome of clinical activity.

At another level, there is also interest in medical audit and peer review. Usually, this results from action by doctors to promote high standards of medical practice. In countries like Canada, audit is essentially a local activity, while in Holland it stems from a national initiative. In West Germany, government has stipulated that medical audit should be undertaken in legislation, and has given responsibility to the sick funds and medical associations for putting this into effect.

Associated with resource management and medical audit, there has been a concern to promote standards and guidelines for service provision. In Holland and Sweden this process has been led by organisations such as the CBO (National Organisation for Quality Assurance in Hospitals) and the Swedish Planning and Rationalisation Institute (SPRI) respectively, and in Canada it has been associated with the work of the Canadian Council on Health Facilities Accreditation. Like the Joint Commission on the Accreditation of Health Care Organisations in the US, the Canadian Council's role is to safeguard the quality of care through visits of survey teams, in the context of explicit standards.

Cutting across a number of these developments has been the growth of managed health care in the United States. Typically, managed care involves closer examination of the appropriateness of treatment decisions through pre-admission certification of patients, concurrent review during treatment, second opinion programmes, and retrospective review after discharge. Utilisation review has also led to the development of protocols for the treatment of particular conditions as a way of limiting the use of tests and procedures. The focus of utilisation review is thus the micro-management of clinical decisions as a strategy for containing costs. HMOs have been at the forefront of managed care and have attached considerable importance to the effective use of resources.

At the macro level, those responsible for funding health services have also taken an increasing interest in the costs and benefits of health care technology. This has given rise to a range of initiatives, including regulating the dissemination of specific technologies, anticipating the future development of technology, and establishing agencies charged with responsibility for technology assessment. While elements of each of these approaches are to be found in the UK, there has not been the same focus of interest as in Holland, Sweden and the United States.

Taken together, resource management, medical audit, the development of standards and guidelines, health services accreditation, managed care and technology assessment represent responses by policy makers to the various problems in the delivery of health care that have emerged in the countries studied. While each country has taken these initiatives to a different stage of development, it is clear that achieving greater effectiveness and efficiency in health services is an issue high on the health policy agenda everywhere. In this sense, the government's plans for the NHS are in step with international developments, although there are some obvious gaps in these plans, particularly in relation to accreditation and technology assessment. In our conclusion, we suggest some ways in which these gaps might be filled.

The second issue relevant to the UK is the concern to shift resources away from institutional care into community care. Sweden offers the closest analogue with the UK, with the Griffiths reforms being matched by plans to transfer responsibility and budgets for non-acute care of elderly people from county councils to municipal councils. The aim of these plans is to enable municipal councils to integrate care of elderly people with their social services responsibilities and to place less reliance on institutional provision. Related developments are taking place in West Germany and Holland where social insurance is being extended to encompass home care for severely disabled people and community care respectively. One of the objectives of these changes is to encourage the substitution of home care and community support for residential services. Similarly, in Canada a number of the provincial governments are seeking to develop services out of hospital in the search for greater cost-effectiveness in service delivery.

Third, in several countries there have been moves to introduce global budgets both for hospitals and for doctors' fees. In the case of hospitals, Canada, Holland, Sweden, the UK and West Germany all employ some form of prospective budgeting, while the United States uses the prospective payments system, based on diagnosis related groups, for Medicare patients. Like global budgets, prospective payment has had a moderating influence on hospital costs. Admissions have fallen, outpatient treatment has been substituted for inpatient care, and there have been reductions in diagnostic tests and procedures. However, the impact on total spending has been limited because prospective payment excludes doctors' fees and care provided out of hospital. Also, prospective payment does nothing to control the quantity of services provided, with the result that hospital spending in the United States remains more open-ended than in countries which rely on global budgets.

In the case of paying doctors, those countries which use a fee-for-service system have taken an increasing interest in global budgets. West Germany has been most effective in this respect and has been able to reconcile fee-for-service reimbursement with cost control by persuading doctors to accept the use of a cap on expenditure on fees. Also, doctors have been prepared to take responsibility for the distribution of the budget. A number of the Canadian provinces are moving in a similar direction. Despite this, the incentives built into fee-for-service reimbursement encourage the over-provision of services, while the structure of the fee schedule skews medical practices in the direction of those services that enhance doctors' incomes. The clear implication for the UK is that fee-for-service payment should be avoided unless there are compelling reasons to suggest otherwise.

More promising in this respect is the development of budgets for doctors in order to reduce the unnecessary use of hospital services. The interest shown in HMOs in the United States and the Bavarian Contract in West Germany parallels proposals for GP budgets in the UK. As experience in these countries indicates, budgets for GPs will have to be designed carefully, both to offer real incentives to GPs to provide care themselves rather than to refer patients to specialists, and to ensure that high standards of practice are maintained. On the basis of United States experience, Weiner and Ferriss (1990) have drawn attention to a number of potential pitfalls in the GP budget holding proposal, and they argue for a period of evaluation in which alternative models are tested.

Public Health

Although there is much rhetoric in support of public health policy, the reality is that the financing and delivery of health *services* continue to dominate health policy debate in all countries. This is well illustrated in the UK where Working for Patients focused principally on acute hospital services and primary care, and ignored the part to be played by public health in the future of the NHS. How can the international neglect of public health be explained?

As Evans (1982) has noted in his analysis of the impact of the Canadian Lalonde Report, a major part of the explanation lies in the wide range of interpretations that can be placed on the causes of mortality and morbidity in contemporary society. In view of the influence of lifestyle, the environment, people's social and economic circumstances and other factors, there are many different ways of seeking to improve health. Depending on the values of the party in government, this can result in campaigns to persuade individuals to alter their lifestyles, attempts to shift investment in health care away from curative services and towards preventive medicine, and action by government to regulate activities outside the health services (for example, the wearing of seatbelts and tobacco and alcohol prices).

It is, of course, possible to use a combination of these approaches, or alternatively to take minimal action by arguing that not enough is known about the precise causes of ill health to enable government to act confidently. The latter position is, however, increasingly untenable, given the magnitude of the challenge posed by new diseases such as AIDS, and the continuing toll of premature mortality attributable to heart diseases, cancers, strokes and accidents. Also, as the impact of health services on health, or at least on widely used health indicators, such as perinatal and infant mortality and life expectancy, is seen to be limited, politicians from both the left and right are turning their attention to other measures in the hope of reducing morbidity and avoidable mortality. Hard evidence about the effectiveness of policies designed to prevent ill health may be lacking, but this has not dampened the enthusiasm of public health advocates for action in this field.

The experience of the countries we have studied suggests that there are three broad approaches available to policy makers seeking to give greater priority to public health. The first, represented most clearly by Sweden, follows closely the WHO's Health for All strategy. This emphasises the social, economic and environmental influences on health, sees government agencies as having a key role in moderating these influences, and attaches high priority to reducing social class differences in health.

A second approach focuses principally on personal behaviour, self care and mutual aid. It is this that has characterised many of the policy initiatives taken in Holland and Canada in recent years. These initiatives also pay some attention to broader societal and environmental influences on health, but the role of the individual and lifestyle factors continue to figure prominently.

The third approach seeks to combine elements of these two strategies. The policies pursued by national and local agencies in the UK fit most readily into this category. Although the Black Report (1980) on inequalities in health was largely ignored by government, there has been an attempt to give greater priority to some preventive health services. This is evident, for example, in the emphasis placed on vaccination and immunisation programmes, and on screening for breast and cervical cancer. At the same time, much of the work of the Health Education Authority, and its predecessor, the Health Education Council, has sought to provide information to individuals to enable them to exercise healthier choices. This is also a key element in the Heartbeat Wales programme. In addition, the programme seeks to stimulate action by a range of agencies including employers and food retailers to reduce heart disease.

At the local level, a number of health authorities and local authorities have endeavoured to adopt a broadly based approach to public health, often involving support for Health for All and the establishment of health targets. The Healthy Cities initiative is an example of this approach. With its emphasis on inter sectoral action to improve health, this initiative closely resembles the policies pursued in Sweden.

As there has been relatively little experience of what has been called "the New Public Health", and even less evaluation, it is impossible to offer a clear judgement on which of the approaches outlined here offers the best way forward. Indeed, at a more fundamental level, it should be noted that the case for giving priority to public health in any of its guises in preference to hospital and other services is to a large extent unproven, certainly in terms of the health benefits likely to result from a given investment of resources. In the same way as health care technologies must be evaluated, so too there needs to be proper assessment of public health programmes to establish their cost effectiveness. As Russell (1986) has shown, contrary to the popular view, prevention usually adds to health service expenditure, and individual measures must be evaluated on their merits to establish where resources can be most effectively applied. Whitehead's review of health education programmes is an example of how this can be done, and further work along similar lines is required (Whitehead, 1989).

Notwithstanding the lack of evidence, the growing interest in public health in the countries we have studied and the multi-causal nature of contemporary health problems suggests that policy makers are increasingly likely to turn their attention to this area in the future. Smith and Jacobson (1988) have argued that a strategy for public health must embrace both personal behaviour and government action and should include explicit goals and targets set at a national level. In this respect, the UK has clearly fallen behind countries like Canada and Sweden where governments have followed the lead set by WHO and produced clearly defined strategies for the promotion of health.

It is also evident that the UK lags behind in the international league table of health indicators. As Table 3 shows, of all the countries in our study, Sweden has the consistently lowest rates of infant and perinatal deaths, and it also performs well in terms of life expectancy at birth. Sweden is followed closely by Holland and then Canada and West Germany. In comparison, both the UK and the United States have relatively poor health records when judged against these indicators. In interpreting these figures, it is worth remembering that most measures of health status are expressed as mean values, and countries with a highly skewed distribution may therefore appear less favourably in these terms.

Table 3   Health Indicators

		UK	SWE	CAN	HOL	WG	USA
Infant mortality rate	Male	12.2	7.1	10.4	9.2	10.6	12.8
	Female	9.4	6.5	7.8	7.5	8.9	10.2
Perinatal Mortality Rate		12.0	7.7	10.7	10.7	10.5	12.6
Life expectancy at birth	Male	71.3	73.5	72.0	73.0	71.3	70.9
	Female	77.3	79.6	79.0	79.8	78.1	78.4

Source: OECD (1985, 1987)

As we have noted, the financing and provision of health services is only one of a number of influences on the health of a country. The importance of what happens outside the health care field is illustrated by comparing Sweden and the United States. It seems likely that a longstanding commitment to social equity and to comprehensive social welfare provision, rather than the more recent interest in public health policy, has made a significant contribution to Sweden's achievement in improving the health of its population. Equally, the wide differences in income and social conditions that are evident in the United States probably help to account for that country's position in relation to other industrialised societies. Despite spending a bigger share of its national income on health services than any other country, and notwithstanding some superb examples of excellence in clinical care for many individuals, the United States has much ground to make up.

In addition, of course, there are major differences in health services between the United States and Sweden. In the United States, access to health services is unequal, with some groups able to call on the full range of services, while others have no cover and are forced to fall back on whatever provision is available to those in need. In Sweden, there is universal coverage through the public system and comprehensive care is available to all. As we showed in chapter 6, Canada is also able to deliver health services to all its population at considerably lower cost than the United States. And like Sweden, Canada has a more impressive health record than the United States.

In short, factors both within the health services and outside appear to be related to a country's health. The absence of reliable evidence on the precise relationship between medical treatment and health outcomes (Wolfe, 1986) means that any judgement in this area must necessarily be tentative. Nevertheless, in the case of health services, it would seem that the overall level of expenditure is less important as an influence on health than the way in which this expenditure is distributed.

Conclusion

As our study has shown, there are no quick-fix solutions to the problems faced by the health care systems of developed countries. Every effort should therefore be made to ensure that experience from one country is evaluated and transferred to other countries to promote the learning process to which we hope to have contributed in this book. In carrying out our investigation, we have been struck by the limited exchange of experience and evidence between countries, and we would argue for higher priority to be given to this activity in the future.

In this conclusion, we summarise our main findings. We also go beyond these findings to reflect on the evidence we have reviewed in order to identify the relevance of overseas experience for the future of the NHS. The systems we have examined are all undergoing or debating reforms of one kind or another, and it is important to keep these reforms under review to establish their implications for health services finance and delivery internationally.

On finance, our principal conclusion is that all methods of funding have their weaknesses. United States experience demonstrates the short-comings of systems that rely mainly on private insurance, and indicates that the real choice facing policy makers is between social insurance and tax funding. If tax funding is to be retained, there is a strong case for increasing expenditure to overcome the shortfall in spending that we have identified. The alternative would be to switch to compulsory social insurance, but this would have to be handled carefully to avoid the difficulties that have arisen elsewhere. Whichever route is taken, it is clear that the way in which resources are used is at least as important as how these resources are raised, indicating the need to examine the delivery of services alongside their financing.

As far as health care delivery is concerned, it is clear that a number of problems recur almost regardless of the method and level of funding. These problems include an over-emphasis on hospital services, evidence of inefficiency in the use of hospitals, the relative neglect of primary care, a lack of incentives for GPs to deal with patients in a primary care setting and poor integration between hospital services, primary care and social care. Governments have attempted to tackle these problems through competition policy in some countries and regulation in others.

Notwithstanding the claims made for these policies, it is important to emphasise that in all countries there is dissatisfaction with the effectiveness of the chosen strategy and a search for new policy instruments. This has led market-oriented systems to make greater use of regulation. Conversely, a number of countries which have traditionally relied on planning and regulation are moving towards a more competitive model.

Our survey indicates that the introduction of competition between providers must be handled carefully if the achievement of the NHS in providing readily accessible specialist services is to be maintained. There is a clear risk that hospitals will respond to the incentives of the market and concentrate on those services that attract resources at the expense of those that do not. This could result in a more fragmented service in which patients have to travel further for treatment. Evidence from the United States demonstrates the weaknesses inherent in a free market in health care, suggesting that managed competition is the most promising way forward (Ham et al., 1989).

A key element of managed competition is likely to be the development of effective purchasers of care. As our review has shown, separating responsibility for funding and provision does not of itself lead to greater efficiency in the use of resources. Neither the provincial governments in Canada nor the sick funds in Holland and West Germany have attached high priority to assessing the way in which hospitals use their budgets. The absence of prudent purchasers in these countries is one of the reasons why there are inefficiencies in service delivery.

In this respect, United States experience of managed care may offer a better pointer to the direction in which services will develop in the UK. As evidence from the United States indicates, it will be essential for health authorities and GP budget holders to use their buying power to exert leverage over providers if the potential benefits of competition are to be realised. It may also be necessary for the government to require hospitals to publish data about their costs, as happens in West Germany, to enable purchasers to make informed choices on behalf of their residents.

A further conclusion to be drawn from the United States is that purchasers will need to monitor treatment decisions to avoid being faced with bills for services of questionable appropriateness. Under the government's plans for the NHS, purchasers and providers will often face different incentives, providers aiming to maximise income through increased activity, and purchasers seeking to avoid unnecessary expenditure to keep within budget. This suggests that utilisation review will receive greater attention, as will work to investigate the effectiveness and appropriateness of clinical care.

As we have noted, this has started to happen in the United States where there is growing interest in the analysis of health outcomes, the study of variations in clinical practice, and assessment of the appropriateness of treatment of specific conditions. This interest, which stems in part from disillusion with competition policy (Quam, 1989), has put the quality of care at the centre of health policy debate. The implication for the UK is that medical audit and the collection and analysis of data about the effectiveness of clinical practices will be key activities for the future. Not least, there will be a demand from consumers for evidence about the quality of services on offer, and a need on the part of purchasers for data to enable them to assess the performance of providers. In this area, as in relation to costs, a uniform method of data collection is essential if performance is to be compared on a systematic basis (Enthoven, 1989).

One of the ways in which work on clinical effectiveness could be taken forward is through the establishment of a national agency charged with responsibility for technology assessment. Agencies of this kind are to be found in Holland, Sweden and the United States, and there have been repeated calls for a similar body to be set up in the UK (see, for example, Jennett, 1986). Such a body would act as a focus for research and analysis into the effectiveness of clinical care, stimulating work by researchers and disseminating the results to the purchasers, providers and consumers of health services.

There may also be a role for an accreditation agency. Experience from overseas suggests that such an agency could play a useful part in promoting good practices and in stimulating providers to raise standards of care. However, this experience also indicates that accreditation needs to move beyond the environment of care to encompass the quality of clinical services; those undertaking accreditation should be independent of service providers; and the emphasis should be less on lengthy checklists of standards than qualitative peer review. The experiments underway in the UK into accreditation will need to incorporate these lessons and ensure that those undertaking reviews of services have access to data to enable the standards of clinical care to be assessed.

Our review has highlighted the importance of global budgets as an instrument for controlling expenditure. The main weakness of global budgets is the lack of rewards for productivity and efficiency. Reconciling overall cost control in hospitals with the provision of incentives for efficiency is a key policy challenge for the future.

This suggests that the work going on as part of the resource management initiative should continue to receive priority. In particular, medical and nursing staff should be encouraged to take greater responsibility for the management of services within agreed budgets and workload agreements. This process should be encouraged through the development of information systems to support resource management and an investment in management development for doctors and nurses. Equally, proposals to give GPs budgets are worth testing, provided that these proposals are designed sensitively and take account of experience gained in the first few years. In this area, as in many other parts of the white paper, there is no substitute for carefully monitored pilot projects.

In view of concern about the private sector playing a bigger part in health care delivery in the UK, it is worth emphasising again that in all of the countries we have studied, apart from Sweden, there is a good deal of pluralism on the supply side (see Table 4). Furthermore, our analysis suggests that as long as the bulk of financing comes from public sources and guarantees access to health care for all, the question of who owns and manages health care facilities is of secondary importance. As Canadian experience indicates, the assumption by government of responsibility for the greater part of funding has been the key factor in ensuring the provision of comprehensive health care to the whole population. It should, however, be noted that the Canadian government prohibits private insurers from offering cover for services included in the public scheme, and this has enabled the government to control expenditure and achieve equitable access.

Table 4 Public and Private Provision

COUNTRY	OWNERSHIP OF HEALTH CARE FACILITIES	EMPLOYMENT AND PAYMENT OF DOCTORS
UK	Mainly public, supplemented by private for-profit and not-for-profit.	Consultants: salaried in public employment and fee-for-service in private practice. GPs: a mixture of salary, capitation and fee-for-service.
SWEDEN	Overwhelmingly public.	Salaried public service.
CANADA	Private not-for-profit.	Mainly fee-for-service with some salaried employment.
HOLLAND	Private not-for-profit.	Consultants: fee-for-service. GPs: capitation and fee-for-service.
WEST GERMANY	Mixture of public and private, both for-profit and not-for-profit.	Mainly fee-for-service out of hospital and salaried in hospitals.
USA	Mainly private, both for-profit and not-for-profit, supplemented by public facilities.	Mainly fee-for-service.

Finally, our discussion of approaches to public health indicates that a variety of strategies have been adopted in different countries. No country can claim to have given public health the same kind of priority that health services have received but there are signs that this is changing. Overseas experience suggests that more effective policy leadership is needed by government if public health is to receive greater attention in the UK. This should be linked to a commitment to evaluate public health programmes to establish their cost effectiveness.

References

H. Aaron and W. Schwartz (1984), *The Painful Prescription: Rationing Hospital Care*, The Brookings Institution, Washington DC.

C. Altenstetter (1986), 'Reimbursement policy of hospitals in the Federal Republic of Germany', *International Journal of Health Planning and Management*, 1:3, 189-211.

C. Altenstetter (1987), 'An end to a consensus on health care in the Federal Republic of Germany', *Journal of Health Politics, Policy and Law*, 12:3, 505-536.

American Hospitals Association (1989), *Hospital Statistics*, 1988 edition, American Hospitals Association, Chicago.

J. Ashton and H. Seymour (1988), *The New Public Health*, Open University Press, Milton Keynes.

Y. Bally (1982), *Incentives for Efficiency in the West German Health Care Sector: The Bavarian Experiment*, Health Economics Research Unit, Discussion Paper No. 04/82, University of Aberdeen.

M.L. Barer et al. (1988), 'Fee Controls as Cost Control: Tales from the Frozen North', *The Milbank Quarterly*, 66:1, 1-63.

F. Beske (1988), 'Federal Republic of Germany' in R. Saltman (ed.), *The International Handbook of Health Care Systems*, Greenwood Press, New York.

Black Report (1980), *Inequalities in Health*, DHSS, London.

R.J. Blendon (1989), 'Three Systems: A Comparative Survey', *Health Managment*, First Quarter, 2-10.

L. Brittan (1988), *A New Deal for Health Care*, Conservative Political Centre, London.

R.H. Brook et al. (1983), 'Does Free Care Improve Adult's Health?', *New England Journal of Medicine*, 309, 1426-34.

E. Butler and M. Pirie (1988), *Health Management Units*, Adam Smith Institute, London.

P. Caper (1988), 'Solving the Medical Care Dilemma', *The New England Journal of Medicine*, 318:32, 1535-1536.

M.R. Chassin et al. (1987), 'Does Inappropriate Use Explain Geographic Variations in the Use of Medical Care Services?', *Journal of the American Medical Association*, 258,2533-37.

S. Christensen, S. Long and J. Rodgers (1987), 'Acute Health Care Costs for the Aged Medicare Population,' *The Milbank Quarterly*, 65:3, 397-493.

M. Dohler (1987), *Regulating the Medical Profession in Germany: The Politics of Efficiency Review*, Social Science Research Centre, Berlin.

A.C. Enthoven (1985), *Reflections on the Managment of the NHS*, Nuffield Provincial Hospitals Trust, London.

A.C. Enthoven (1988), *Theory and Practice of Managed Competition in Health Care Finance*, Elsevier, Amsterdam.

A.C. Enthoven (1989), *Management Information and Analysis for the Swedish Health Care System*, The Swedish Institute for Health Economics, Lund.

A.C. Enthoven and R. Kronick (1989), 'A Consumer-Choice Health Plan for the 1990s', *The New England Journal of Medicine*, 320:1, 29-37.

J. Epp (1986), *Achieving Health for All: A Framework for Health Promotion*, Minister of Supply and Services, Canada.

J.R. Evans (1987), *Towards a Shared Direction for Health in Ontario*, Report of the Ontario Health Review Panel.

R. Evans (1982), 'A Retrospective on the "New Perspective"', *Journal of Health Politics, Policy and Law*, 7:2, 325-344.

R. Evans (1984), *Strained Mercy*, Butterworths, Toronto.

R. Evans (1986), 'Finding the Levers, Finding the Courage: Lessons from Cost Containment in North America', *Journal of Health Politics, Policy and Law*, 11:4, 585-615.

R. Evans (1988), 'Split Vision: Interpreting Cross-Border Differences in Health Spending' *Health Affairs*, Winter, 17-24.

R. Evans et al. (1989), 'Controlling Health Expenditures — The Canadian Reality', *The New England Journal of Medicine*, 320:9, 571-7.

M. Goldsmith and D. Willetts (1988), *Managed Health Care: A New System For A Better Health Service*, Centre for Policy Studies, London.

W.A. Glaser (1987), *Paying the Hospital. The Organisation, Dynamics and Effects of Differing Financial Arrangements*, Jossey-Bass, San Francisco.

D. Green (1986), *Challenge to the NHS*, Institute of Economic Affairs, London.

S. Hakansson (1986), 'Frame Budgets in Sweden' in L. Paine (ed.), *International Hospital Federation Official Yearbook 1986*, Sabrecrown Publishing, London.

C.J. Ham (1987), *Steering the Oil Tanker: Power and Policy Making in the Swedish Health Service*, King's Fund Institute, London.

C.J. Ham et al. (1989), *Managed Competition*, King's Fund Institute, Briefing Paper 9, London.

K.D. Henke (1989), 'The Health Care System of the Federal Republic of Germany' in *Advances in Health Economics and Health Services Research*, Supplement, 1989, Health Care Systems in Ten Industrial Countries.

F.A. Ievins and B. Revenas (1990), 'Decentralising Health Care in Sweden', *British Medical Journal*, 300, 6.

J.K. Iglehart (1986), 'Canada's Health Care System', *The New England Journal of Medicine*, 315:3, 202-208, 315:12, 778-784, and 315:25, 1623-1628.

B. Jennett (1986), *High Technology Medicine*, Oxford University Press, New Edition, Oxford.

T. Jost (1990), *Assessing the Quality of Medical Practice: An International Comparative Study*, King's Fund, London.

R. Jowell et al. (1988), *British Social Attitudes: the 5th Report*, Gower, Aldershot.

B. Kirkmann-Liff and W. van de Ven (1989), 'Improving Efficiency in the Dutch Health Care System: Current Innovations and Future Options', *Health Policy*, 13, 35-53.

Lalonde Report (1974), *A New Perspective on the Health of Canadians*, Ministry of National Health and Welfare, Ottawa.

Landstingsforbundet (1988), *Bevare mig val...*, Stockholm.

R. Lapre (1988), 'A Change of direction in the Dutch Health Care System?', *Health Policy*, 10, 21-32.

D. LeTouze (1986), 'The Canadian Health Care System: At the Crossroads', *World Hospitals*, xxii:i, 7-13.

J. Lomas et al. (1989), 'Paying Physicians in Canada: Minding Our Ps and Qs', *Health Affairs*, 8:1, 80-102.

H. Luft (1985), 'Competition and Regulation', *Medical Care*, 23:5, 383-400.

H. Luft et al. (1986), 'The Role of Specialised Clinical Services in Competition Among Hospitals', *Inquiry*, 23, 83-94.

G. McLachlan and A. Maynard (eds) (1982), *The Public/Private Mix for Health*, Nuffield Provincial Hospitals Trust, London.

J.A.M. Maarse (1989), 'Hospital budgeting in Holland: aspects, trends and effects', *Health Policy*, 11, 257-276.

R.J. Maxwell (1981), *Health and Wealth*, Lexington Books, Lexington, Massachusetts.

R.J. Maxwell (1988), 'Financing Health Care: Lessons from Abroad', *British Medical Journal*, 296, 1423-6.

G. Melnick and J. Zwanziger (1988), 'Hospital Behaviour Under Competition and Cost-Containment Policies: The California Experience, 1980 to 1985', *Journal of the American Medical Association*, 260:18, 2669-75.

Ministry of Welfare, Health and Cultural Affairs (1986), *Health 2000*, Rijswijk.

NAHA (1987), *Autumn Survey 1987*, Birmingham.

National Board of Health and Welfare (1982), *Health in Sweden*, Stockholm.

National Board of Health and Welfare (1985), *The Swedish Health Services in the 1990s*, Stockholm.

National Board of Health and Welfare (1988), *Public Health Report*, Stockholm.

J.P. Newhouse et al. (1981), 'Some Interim Results From a Controlled Trial of Cost Sharing Health Insurance', *New England Journal of Medicine*, 305,1501.

J.P. Newhouse et al. (1988), 'Hospital Spending in the United States and Canada: A Comparison', *Health Affairs*, Winter, 6-16.

OECD (1987), *Financing and Delivering Health Care*, OECD, Paris.

M. Pauly (1989), 'Efficiency, Equity and Costs in the US Health Care Systems' in C. Havinghurst, R. Helms, C. Bladen and M. Pauly (eds), *American Health Care, What are the lessons for Britain?*, Institute of Economic Affairs, London.

L. Pine et al. (1988), 'The Swedish Medical Care Programme: An Interim Assessment', *Health Policy*, 10, 155-176.

G.T. Pollock (1989), 'Hospital Departments of Community Health — the Quebec Approach to the Organisation of Health Promotion', *Public Health*, 103, 11-14.

J.P. Poullier and G.J. Schieber (1988), 'International Health Care Expenditure and Utilisation Trends: An Update', *Health Affairs*, 7:4, 104-112.

J.E. Powell (1976), *Medicine and Politics: 1975 and After*, Pitman Medical, Tunbridge Wells.

L. Quam (1989), 'Improving Clinical Effectiveness in the NHS: An Alternative to the White Paper', *British Medical Journal*, 229, 448-50.

M. Rachlis and C. Kushner (1989), *Second Opinion*, Collins, Toronto.

J. Raeburn (1987), 'Options for Health Promotion: What Can We Learn From the Canadians?', *New Zealand Health Review*, 6:4, 21-24.

M. Raffel and N. Raffel (1989), *The US System: Origins and Functions*, John Wiley and Sons, 3rd edition, New York.

R. Robinson et al. (1988), *Health Finance: Assessing the Options*, King's Fund Institute Briefing Paper 4, London

M. Rosenthal (1986), 'Beyond Equity? Swedish Health Policy and the Private Sector', *The Milbank Quarterly*, 64:4, 592-621.

L.B. Russell (1986), *Is Prevention Better than Cure?*, The Brookings Institution, Washington D.C.

F. Rutten and D. Banta (1988), 'Health Care Technologies in the Netherlands', *International Journal of Technology Assessment in Health Care*, 4, 229-238.

F. Rutten and A. van der Werff (1982), 'Health Policy in the Netherlands', in G. McLachlan and A. Maynard (eds) *The Public/Private Mix for Health*, The Nuffield Provincial Hospitals Trust, London.

R. Saltman and A. de Roo, (1989), 'Hospital Policy in the Netherlands: The Parameters of Structural Stalemate', *Journal of Health Politics, Policy and Law*, 14:4, 1-23.

R. Saltman and C. von Otter (1987), 'Revitalizing Public Health Care Systems: A Proposal For Public Competition In Sweden', *Health Policy*, 9:1, 21-40.

R. Saltman and C. von Otter (1989), 'Public Competition Versus Mixed Markets: An Analytic Comparison', *Health Policy*, 11: 1, 43-55.

G.J. Schieber and J.P. Poullier (1989), 'International Health Care Expenditure Trends: 1987', *Health Affairs*, 8:3, 169-177.

F.T. Schut and W. van de Ven (eds) (1987), *Proceedings of the Conference on Regulated Competition in the Dutch Health Care System*, Erasmus University, Rotterdam.

J.M.G. Schulenburg (1983), 'Report from Germany: Current Controversies in the Health Care System', *Journal of Health Politics, Policy and Law*, 8:2, 320-351

Secretary of State for Health and Others (1989), *Working for Patients*, HMSO, London.

A. Smith and B. Jacobson (eds) (1988), *The Nation's Health*, King's Fund, London.

R.A. Spasoff (1987), *Health for All Ontario*, Report of the Panel on Health Goals for Ontario.

H.M. Stevenson et al. (1988), 'Medical Politics and Canadian Medicare: Professional Response to the Canada Health Act', *The Milbank Quarterly*, 66:1, 65-104.

G. Stoddart and D. Feeny (1986), 'Policy Options for Health Care Technology' in D. Feeny et al., (eds), *Health Care Technology: Effectiveness, Efficiency and Public Policy*, Institute for Research on Public Policy, Montreal.

A. Stoline and J.P. Weiner (1988), *The New Medical Market Place: A Physician's Guide to the Health Care Revolution*, The Johns Hopkins University Press, Baltimore.

Sunnybrook Report (1988), *Symposium on Organisational Models for Involving the Physician in Management*, Sunnybrook Medical Centre, Toronto.

G. Unge (Personal Communication), Interview held on 23 November 1988, Stockholm.

W. van de Ven (1987), 'The Key Role of Health Finance in a Cost-Effective Health Care System', *Health Policy*, 7, 253-272.

N. Weaver (1988), *Consideration of The Canadian Medical Chief of Staff Role and its Suitability to the UK*, King's Fund Travelling Fellowhsip.

D. Webber (1988), 'The "Old Man" Blum and the Health Insurance "Sea": The Conflict over the health insurance reform in the Federal Republic of Germany, 1987-1988', Max Planck Institute, Cologne, Unpublished Paper.

J. Weiner and D. Ferriss (1990), *GP Budget Holding in the UK*, King's Fund Institute Research Report 7, London.

J. Wennberg (1987), 'Population Illness Rates Do Not Explain Population Hospitalisation Rates', *Medical Care*, 25:4, 354-9.

M. Whitehead (1989), *Swimming Upstream*, King's Fund Institute, Research Report 5, London.

B.L. Wolfe (1986), 'Health Status and Medical Expenditures: Is There a Link?', *Social Science and Medicine*, 22:10, 993-999.